Listings

D0248754

About the author

Julius Honnor is a writer, editor and photographer who lived and worked in Verona after finishing a degree in philosophy, teaching English in one of its schools. His other Italian experiences include working on campsites. He wrote Footprint's guide to Naples and has contributed text to guidebooks on London, Berlin and the UK, and photos to several more, including Bologna and Turin. Born and brought up on the edge of Dartmoor he has travelled the world, taught foreign kids in a Yorkshire village, designed web pages, worked in bookshops in Plymouth and Kensington, helped build systems for an internet publisher and played lots of football along the way.

Acknowledgements

Thanks to Silvia, Patrizia, Michela for kind hospitality and especially to David for copious hospitality and wine, and stories and limericks. Thanks to Chiara for lunch and good suggestions. Thanks to Ryan for some useful research on rides and getting wet. Thanks to Hannah and Sam for complicated orders and table tennis talk. Most of all, thanks to Clair for visits and phone calls, moral support and the watering of plants.

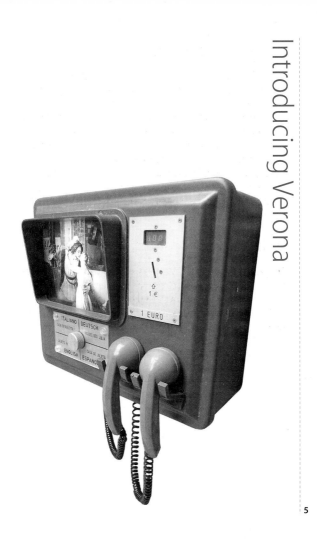

Red-roofed and pastel-shaded, Verona sits in a bend of the river Adige as it winds its way south from the Alps. On the edge of the mountains and the cusp of the plain, the city likes to think of itself as both the beginning and the distillation of the real Italy. At the Italian crossroads of the north-south route from the Brenner Pass to Rome and the east-west Milan-Venice road, it is easy to see the reasons for the city's long-standing strategic importance. The self-importance is harder to explain, but is due in part to an extraordinary architectural, artistic, agricultural and financial wealth. Apart from Rome itself, Verona is Italy's best-preserved Roman city, with a Roman amphitheatre, a Roman bridge, Roman gates and a Roman theatre all providing prominent symbols. Atop these ancient foundations is a richly decorated and well preserved Romanesque, Gothic and Renaissance city, with spectacular frescoed churches and houses. The antiquity is given an opulent sheen by a well-dressed 21st-century population who have, in the main, done very nicely out of wine, opera, European integration and a select brand of tourism.

A night at the opera

With a spectacular 20,000-seat performance space in the very heart of the city, Verona has become justly famous for its summer opera season. Enormous, lavish productions take place every night during the summer months, the audience sitting with candles on the original Roman stone seats of the amphitheatre. Outside of the opera season the Arena is also used for pop concerts. The Roman theatre to the north of the river stages some top-notch theatre productions and there's a varied musical programme of modern, classical and jazz at other locations around the city. Balancing out Verona's somewhat staid reputation, the university influences a more youthful and vibrant side to the arts scene, and there's alternative music and art to be found, too.

Grapes of wealth

Verona is more than just the sum of its arts. The city is an important trade centre and more goods now pass through its venerable old portals than the port of Genoa. Wine is also key to the city's wealth. The vine carpeted slopes of the Valpolicella and Soave regions rise up on either side of the city, which, not surprisingly, plays host to *Vinitaly*, the country's top wine fair. Olives, too, grow in abundance in the fecund hills to the north, east and west, while, to the equally fertile south, beyond a sprawling industrial area, the Po plain is an enormous patchwork of crop-yielding fields.

Renaissance city

The crasser side of Verona's tourism centres on a bizarrely contrived Romeo and Juliet trail around a series of fictional sites. The city's real and multi-layered history, meanwhile, is more interesting, and apparent everywhere you turn. From the Romans to Mussolini via an unlikely 4th-century African patron saint, and the great artists and architects of the Renaissance, Verona's streets, houses, churches and piazzas combine to tell the fascinating story of this small, but hugely significant, northern Italian city.

At a glance

Centro storico

Bordered on three sides by the river Adige, the streets of Verona's
ancient centre follow the layout of the Roman city. Most of the
well-known sights are still here, between Ponte Pietra, the bridge
which predates the city, in the north, along narrow winding streets
and across piazzas to the original Roman gates of Porta Leoni in
the south and Porta Borsari in the west. The Roman *decumanus
maximus* (main north-south road) still exists in corso Porta Borsari
and corso Sant'Anastasia. It intersects with the *cardo maximus* at
the site of the Roman forum, now piazza Erbe, the beautiful heart
of the city and just one of a cluster of wonderful piazzas.

Piazza dei Signori, leading off piazza Erbe, is more refined, and
equally beautiful. While the foundations are Roman, much of what
sits on top is Gothic, Romanesque and Renaissance and narrow
streets of ancient palazzi, many still frescoed, stretch up to the
Adige. The Duomo, the city's cathedral, is just one of many
spectacular churches. The stamp of the medieval rulers, the della
Scala family, is visible most ostentatiously in their elaborate Gothic
tombs. Also here are the city's main shopping streets, including the
shiny pedestrianized via Mazzini, the marble slabs polished by
many thousands of feet which travel its length as much for the
passegiata (the traditional evening stroll) as for the shops.

South of the centro storico

Heading south and west from the original *centro storico,* the city
opens out across piazza Bra and beyond, stretching along the river
as it curves upstream to the west, and down the grand corso Porta
Nuova to the station and the industrial area beyond. The city walls
were extended to include the vast Arena (the amphitheatre) in the
3rd century AD. Just to the northwest of piazza Bra is
Castelvecchio: a castle and bridge providing the city with more of

View from the balcony
Look down on the waves of camera-clicking visitors who sweep in and out of the courtyard at the Casa di Giulietta.

its distinctive icons. Further west, the handsome church of San Zeno is the city's most admired building.

North and east of the Adige

The steep hill of San Pietro was the original site of settlement in the city. At its base, looking out across the river, sits the Roman theatre, and from its top are fantastic panoramic views over the city. To either side of the hill are residential areas of the old city. Though the sights are well spread out here, there are some atmospheric little districts of winding streets, especially in Veronetta to the south, home to many of the city's best bars and restaurants. Beyond rise hills of olives and vineyards, with the first signs of the Alps to the north.

Around Verona

To the northwest of the city, Lake Garda is Italy's biggest and most popular lake. At its wider southern end it is overdeveloped, and a destination for package holidays. Further north, however, high hills enclose it on both sides, increasing its beauty and stifling development. Between the lake and the city is Valpolicella, a hilly wine-growing area. To the north the Parco Naturale Regionale della Lessinia is high and wild enough to make skiing possible in winter and walking popular in summer. It is an area dominated by its stone, whether it be mountainous outcrops, marble quarries, roofs or fenceposts. The Val d'Adige separates Valpolicella and Lessinia from the high ridge Monte Baldo to the west, and Lake Garda beyond. Soave to the east, and the southern plains are more fertile agricultural areas, spotted with villas and villages, many with excellent restaurants, especially around the Mincio river which flows south from the Lake. Further east, Vicenza is a smart town with a *centro storico* full of the work of the great architect Palladio. Mantova to the south has lakes and a small but perfectly-formed medieval centre. Brescia to the west has a castle, more medieval piazzas and some Roman remains among its fascist and modern architecture.

Trip planner

Verona is never overrun with tourists in the way Venice or Florence
are, though it claims to be Italy's fourth most visited city. It can get
pretty busy during the opera season and there is also a big influx of
visitors during the *Vinitaly* trade fair. A clement climate means
spring and autumn are usually warm and sunny. Hot summers are
dotted with occasional spectacular thunderstorms. In winter cold
foggy weather can sit over the Po plain for long stretches but there
is equally the chance of beautifully cold and crisp weather.

24 hours

Start the day with a cappuccino or macchiato and a cornetto (a
sweet croissant) and watch the world go by from a café on or around
the piazza Erbe, the buzzing heart of the city. If you want to check
out Juliet's (supposed) house without the pleasure of the company
of hordes of tourists, head down via Cappello to get there early.
Otherwise find your bearings by walking (or taking the lift) to the top
of the Torre dei Lamberti, with excellent views down to piazza Erbe
and piazza dei Signori below, and across the city. After the long
climb back down you may want to rest on the steps of the Loggia del
Consiglio in piazza dei Signori, Verona's most elegant square. Check
to see if there's anything worth seeing at the Centro Internazionale
di Fotografia, which is also here, off the adjoining cortile del
Tribunale amongst Roman excavations. To the north of piazza dei
Signori the spectacular, Gothic Scaligeri tombs can easily be
appreciated from outside their 14th-century wrought iron enclosure.
Also have a look inside the small but atmospheric church of Santa
Maria Antica, the Scaligeri's erstwhile chapel. Continue in this
direction to explore the narrow streets of the northern end of the
centro storico, especially via Sottoriva, once the centre of
disreputable Verona, now a residential street with several good
cafés, restaurants, bars and shops in its arches. Beyond here is the
river Adige and beautiful Ponte Pietra, the city's oldest construction.

★ **Ten of the best**

1 **Ponte Pietra** The city's oldest and most romantic structure is this bridge over the river Adige.

2 **Piazza Erbe** Away from the city's Roman performance spaces, the human dramas of everyday life still happen here, on the beautiful site of the original forum.

3 **Torre dei Lamberti** By far the best views of the city can be had from the top of the tower in its very centre.

4 **Veronetta** A welcome respite from the city's smart centre, Veronetta has no obvious sights, but plenty of atmosphere and good bars and restaurants.

5 **Arena** The city's largest landmark is still its Roman amphitheatre, standing proud in piazza Bra and used for regular concerts and opera performances.

6 **Giardino Guisti** The gardens of the Palazzo Guisti remain much as they were at their Renaissance inception, complete with intricate box hedges, tall cypresses and great views.

7 **Casa di Giulietta** Tacky and crowded, graffitied and over-photographed, Juliet's house is a blatant tourist trap but absolutely unmissable.

8 **Galleria d'Arte Moderna** A permanent collection featuring some excellent international pieces and an interesting calendar of temporary exhibitions, all in a stunning modern conversion of an ancient palazzo.

9 **Via Sottoriva** Once a place of infamy and ill-repute, Verona's most beautiful street is now home to a groovy collection of bars, shops, galleries and restaurants.

10 **Centro Internazionale di Fotografia** Great photography exhibitions and Roman excavations all rolled into one.

The ★ symbol used throughout the guide indicates recommended sights

If there's time before lunch, have a look at the Duomo, Verona's cathedral, especially its ancient ornate facade. Some of the best little restaurants and *trattorie* are in this area, so pick one for a traditional Veronesi lunch of pasta or polenta - with or without the horsemeat. In the afternoon head to piazza Bra and the Arena, the spectacular Roman amphitheatre, unless you have tickets for an evening opera, in which case you might want to visit the verdant Giardino Guisti or the church of San Zeno in the city's southwest. You should also try to include a stroll across the crenellated bridge of Castelvecchio, and, if there's time, a visit to the museum inside the castle itself. Once the shops reopen around four, you could also stroll up the smart, shiny via Mazzini or the ancient corso Porta Borsari, stopping for a good look at the Porta itself, and perhaps for a coffee or an ice-cream somewhere along the way. After supper, if there's no opera, you could take in some classical music or jazz at the Teatro Filarmonico, or find a bar with some live music and good wine to last long into the night.

A long weekend
An extra couple of days in the city gives the opportunity to explore more leisurely, taking in some of the less obvious parts of the city such as Veronetta, and perhaps a walk into the hills to the north. There are plenty more churches to explore, notably Sant'Anastasia, as well as the Teatro Romano and the Museo Archeologico on the river's left bank.

A week
You could explore a different church, museum and Roman remain every day if you so wished, but in the likely event of history-overload, head for the vineyards of Valpolicella, the Lessini hills or the lapping shores of Lake Garda for a bit of natural beauty and relaxation. Alternatively, Brescia, Vicenza or Mantova offer different slants on cities of the Veneto.

Very Verona
A typically Romanesque Veronese house front on Plazzetta Antonio Titabosco.

Contemporary Verona

On the surface Verona exists very contentedly as a rich and beautiful city enjoying a charmed life in an auspicious position, near a lake, mountains and a fertile plain. Such privilege has bred complacency and the city is seen as being pompous and cold. In Italy's south, Verona is the one northern city which above all others is laughed at and hated in equal measure.

A conservative attitude to life has served Verona well for thousands of years: there is almost no new architecture in the city centre and traditions are held in high esteem. But well hidden beneath the glossy marble veneer of middle class Verona there are tensions created by a conservative opposition to change; contradictions and uncertainties about the future of a city which lives somewhat awkwardly off both its past and its present. And while the city benefits economically from its position in Europe – both touristically and commercially – there is a reluctance to accept the idea of European unity, even at the level of decisions by the European Court of Justice.

While Italian Prime Minister Silvio Berlusconi attempts to pass legislation giving immunity to prosecution for all parliamentarians, including himself, and continues to fight extradition to Spain, Verona's university is at the centre of a now infamous, and typically Italian, battle against corruption and discrimination. Scot David Petrie, an English language lecturer at the university, started his long legal battle against the Italian State in the 1990s. Working at the University of Verona as a self-employed teacher since 1984, Petrie realized that he was doing the same job as Italians but without the same benefits or prospects. The Italian system barred foreign lecturers from receiving insurance contributions and from applying for certain posts. To Petrie and others it was clear the university was in breach of fundamental European anti-discrimination laws guaranteeing freedom of movement for workers and mutual recognition of qualifications.

With support from Scottish MEP Hugh McMahon, Petrie took 65 students and lecturers (including writer Tim Parks, see p229) from the University of Verona to the European Parliament in Strasbourg and petitioned the then president, Egon Klepsch. The response of Verona University was to try to 'disappear' the complainants. Names were withdrawn from internal phone books and from the official website, and 13 teachers were moved into a basement office with only two desks. On 13 July 1995, in an emergency debate in Strasbourg, the European Parliament passed a resolution criticizing Verona for human rights abuses. It remains the only Italian institution ever to have been condemned in this way.

Petrie has now won an unprecedented four EU decisions at the European Court of Justice on the basis of freedom of movement, each one more damning than the last. The story has had massive international coverage, including the front pages of the Wall Street Journal and the Times Educational Supplement, but still the Italian State continues to avoid compliance. The saga has become something of a test case for the rights of European workers, and of the ability of the European Union to enforce European law. The latest ruling threatened Italy with massive fines for every day that they did not comply. Petrie, the 400 or so members of the union he set up for foreign lecturers in Italy and many international observers await the Italians' response.

Illustrating the tensions between tradition and modernity from a different angle is an issue which has taken up many hours of heated conversation over coffee in the city recently. It concerns the *banchetti* (stalls) in piazza Erbe. Superficially trivial, the debate is a microcosm of modern Veronese problems. The place of commerce in the modern city is an ambiguous one. It is common to hear the tutting of Veronesi at the 'tatty' exteriors of some of the city's buildings and there is a risk that gentrification will detract from the city's spirit. Still to be found on many postcards, the old market in the piazza had distinctive large shady umbrellas which had become one of Verona's visual trademarks. Sitting as it did on the site of the original Roman forum, the market had historical roots that went very deep. The argument against the stalls was that they had become unsightly, were poorly maintained and selling cheap tourist tat which lowered the tone of the area. In actual fact the market sold a mixture of fruit and vegetables, snack food, and various other bits and pieces, including tacky souvenirs. The market was removed, leaving a newly gleaming piazza where it was suddenly easier to appreciate the beauty of the place and its surrounding buildings. Piazza delle Erbe, however, had lost some of its heart. The solution eventually agreed by the city council was to make new stalls which would be removed at weekends. However, the logistics of how this would be achieved were not properly thought through. The *Arena*, the local paper, reported that when the first stall reappeared, its tenant was almost certain to be Tina Vitale, *Tina dei carciofi* (Tina of the artichokes), 'true and proper flag' of the stall-holders. In the event, when the first stall finally appeared, it sold Venetian masks, naked lady cigarette lighters and 'Romeo loves Giulietta' baseball caps. Tina and her artichokes were nowhere to be seen.

Easy and cheap to get to, and small enough to get around, Verona is blessed with a relative absence of transport problems. At the crossroads of major north-south and east-west routes it's also exceptionally well-connected to the rest of Italy, making it an ideal stepping stone for a variety of itineraries. Ryanair's cheap flights to nearby Brescia, with a connecting bus service, have increased the city's popularity, and BA flights to Verona have also come down in price. Overland, the train journey from Northern Europe is long but spectacular, as is the drive. Though it's small enough to walk around, cycling is another option, especially in the semi-pedestrianized old Roman centre. For exploring the mountains and countryside around the city, hiring a car might be the best option as public transport is patchy. Lake Garda, however, can get seriously clogged up with traffic during holidays and at weekends, and catching a boat is a more civilized, and often quicker, way of getting from 'A' to 'B'. Tours around the city include walking tours and visits to local *osterie*.

Getting there

Air

From Europe **Ryanair**'s twice daily flights (daily in winter) from London Stansted to Verona (or more acurately to Brescia, see next page) have opened up the city as a long weekend destination for British travellers. **British Airways** compete with this service by offering twice daily flights between London Gatwick and Verona. Ryanair's flights have been known to sell for under £10 each, plus taxes. More usual return prices range between £50 and £200, depending on season and time of the week. In high season, charter flights are also a possibility, as are packages, especially to Lake Garda. Flights from Verona to other European cities include Paris, Frankfurt, Madrid and Vienna.

From North America There are no direct flights from North America to Verona. It is possible either to change at Rome for a connecting flight or to get a flight to Milan and catch the train. **Air Dolomiti** and **Meridiana** both connect to flights from New York, via Rome, Frankfurt and Munich. Prices start at around $650 return. Flying via London is usually cheaper. Total journey times are around ten hours to the East Coast of America.

From Australia and New Zealand **Qantas** fly from Brisbane to Rome (a 26-hour journey), from where you can catch a connecting flight to Verona, but you may find there are more options and lower prices available by flying to London and changing there.

Airport information Getting to and from **Verona Villafranca** airport (also known as Valerio Catullo, **T** 045 8095666, www.aeroportoverona.it) is a fairly simple affair – blue APTV buses run every 20 minutes from the train station, 0700-2335. There is also one at 0005. The journey takes around 15 minutes and costs

→ Airlines and agents

Alitalia T 0874 5448259, www.alitalia.it
British Airways T 0845 7733377, www.britishairways.com
Ryanair T 0871 2460000, www.ryanair.com

Other websites
www.airline-network.co.uk
www.cheapflights.com
www.ebookers.com
www.expedia.com
www.holiday.co.uk
www.statravel.com
www.trailfinders.com
www.travelocity.com

€4.20 each way. During important trade fairs this service extends to the Fiera. Taxis cost around €20 to the centre of the city. The airport has six car rental companies (see directory, p214), a bank, a bar, and a couple of shops.

Tiny **Brescia Montichiari** airport (also known as Gabriele D'Annunzio, **T** 030 9656511, www.aeroportobrescia.it) , used by Ryanair (and called by them, somewhat disingenuously, 'Verona Brescia'), is about an hour away from Verona by bus. Ryanair run a service between the airport and Verona train station which coordinates with their flights and costs €9 single, €16 return. Tickets are available from an office inside the arrivals/departures hall (or, on the return journey from Verona, on the bus). There is a similar service to Brescia.

Car

Verona is just to the northeast of the major junction of the A4 Milan-Venice motorway (European route E70) and the north-south A22 (European route E45 north through the Alps to the Brenner Pass and Innsbruck). Coming from the north take the exit 'Verona Nord' and then the 'tangenziale' in the direction 'centro'. On the A22, take the exit for 'Verona Centro Storico'.

Coach

Eurolines operate three services a week from London Victoria to Verona, changing at Milan and taking around 24 hours. Prices are around £110 return, but only £52 if booked 30 days in advance. Cheap advance fares are not available over Christmas or during July and August. Long distance buses arrive and depart in Verona at the bus station, opposite the train station. **T** 08705 808080 (from the UK), www.nationalexpress.com

Train

There is a direct overnight train from Paris Bercy to Verona which takes around 9 hours . Prices start at about £130 for a mid-week 'leisure return'. London to Paris on **Eurostar** adds another £59 for a mid-week journey. Book or find details through **Rail Europe T** 0870 5848848 (from UK), www.raileurope.co.uk General train information in Italy, **T** 848 888088 (0700-2100), www.trenitalia.com

Getting around

Bus

Orange **AMT** buses serve the city, while blue **APTV** buses go further afield – to Valpolicella, Lake Garda, Soave, Lessinia and Valeggio sul Mincio. All services centre on the sprawling bus station, opposite the train station, south of piazza Bra. Tickets must be bought before boarding, though this is usually waived in the evenings or outside of the city. The nearest ticket outlet should be marked on information boards at bus stops under 'Rivendita biglietti più vicina'. Tickets should be stamped on board, after which they are valid on any bus for one hour.

The most useful city services are likely to be 11, 12, 13, and 14 between the station (from beside the AMT booth) and piazza Bra, continuing over the river to via XX Settembre. At weekends and on holidays these are replaced by services 91, 92 and 98.

There is an AMT ticket and information booth at the station (*Mon-Sat 0630-1300, first and last 3 working days of the month 0630-1250, 1300-1920*) as well as ticket machines, though these are usually broken. Otherwise all *tabacchi* (tobacconists, marked with a large 'T' outside) sell tickets. An ordinary ticket costs €0.93. A 10-journey ticket ('*una tessera*') is also available for €8.70, and a day-ticket ('*giornaliero*') for €3.10. AMT, **T** 045 8871111, www.amt.it

The APTV office (in a separate building opposite the station building) is open *Mon-Sat 0600-2000, Sun 0630-2000* (**T** 045 8057811). Timetables are available online for all routes at www.apt.vr.it in pdf form for you to save or print out. Otherwise they are also available from the main office (above) or from tourist information offices. Bus route 62-64 goes from Verona up the eastern side of Lake Garda to Riva approximately every hour, taking around an hour and a quarter to reach Torri, two hours to reach Torbole. Some buses on this route usefully have a display which informs what the next stop is. Bus 60 goes to Valeggio every hour or so and takes just under an hour. Bus 30 goes to Caldiero (for the Terme di Giunone) and Soave every hour or so, and takes 45 minutes to Soave, half an hour to Caldiero. Various, but rather infrequent, buses head north into the hills of Lessinia. Most useful are probably the 5-6 to Molina and the 10 to Bosco Chiesanuova. Buses are fairly reliable and tickets are cheap, ranging between €0.80 and €5.50.

→ VeronaCard

For €12, VeronaCard offers free use of buses within the city and free entry into most of Verona's museums, monuments and churches, with reduced-price entry into a few others, for a three day period. There is also a one-day version available for €8. The cards are on sale at participating museums, monuments and churches or from some tobacconists. Even if you don't plan to use the cards, the leaflet advertising them contains a very useful map and list of attractions.

Car
Verona is small enough, the streets are narrow enough and the traffic restrictions strict enough, to make driving around the city unnecessary and inefficient. The only reason to hire a car would be to explore the surrounding lakes and mountains, for which public transport is a much less feasible option. For car hire see p214.

Cycling
Verona's semi-pedestrianized centre is good for cycling, though the minute you hit a proper road you won't find drivers giving you much space or respect. For cycle hire see p214.

Taxi
The times you're most likely to want a taxi are when going to and from the station or airport, to the Fiera, or to one of the out-of-town clubs. Prices from the centre of Verona to the station are around €10, to Verona airport €20 and to Brescia airport €85. Radio Taxis, **T** 045 532 666. It's not necessary to pre-book taxis – ring a few minutes before you need one.

Train

Trains go to the southern tip of Lake Garda at Peschiera. Frequent trains also head further west to Brescia and Milan, south to Mantova, Bologna, Florence and Rome, east to Vicenza, Padua and Venice and north to Trento and Bolzano.

Apart from maybe Rome, just about any of these places are feasible as day trips, and the relatively low cost of Italian train travel makes them doubly worthwhile. www.trenitalia.com has good information and timetables for all Italian services and it's possible to buy tickets online. Timetables are printed daily in *Arena*, Verona's newspaper.

Walking

The compact size of Verona's centre means that walking is by far the best way to get around and see the sights. Traffic restrictions in the *centro storico* also mean it's reasonably safe and quiet. Outside of this area you need to be more careful. Though traffic generally respects red lights, pedestrian crossings without lights mean almost nothing. If you can get onto them before a car comes, however, drivers are marginally less likely to mow you down.

Tours

Associazione Culturale Guide Center Verona, via Lungadige Porta Vittoria 23, **T/F** 045 8018175, www.turismoverona.it Fairly standard but informative walking tours of the city, in either 2½- or 5-hour versions. Tours of the vineyards of the Valpolicella and the sights of the Lessinia mountains are among others on offer.

Città Nascosta, via Leoncino 13, **T** 045 8009086. *Mon-Fri 0930-1230, Mon, Wed, Fri, 1530-1830*. Meaning 'Hidden City', Città Nascosta offer tours of lesser-known Verona, and sometimes have access to monuments outside normal opening hours.

Associazione Culturale Quirino Sacchetti, **T** 339 5898238, **F** 045 567824, quirinos@hotmail.com A group promoting the "lesser known aspects of Veronese culture", Quirino Sacchetti (named after a 20th-century poet and artist) organize walking tours lasting about an hour and a half which involve visits to local *osterie* and a certain amount of wine-consumption.

Juliet & Co, **T/F** 045 8103173, www.julietandco.com *Apr-Sep, Mon-Sun 1730*. From April to September Juliet & Co conduct daily walking tours in English of Verona's *centro storico*. The starting point is by the equestrian statue of Vittorio Emanuele II in piazza Bra and the tour lasts 1¼ hours. No reservation needed. €10, children free.

Tourist information

Main Verona information office: via degli Alpini 9, **T** 045 8068680, **F** 045 8003638, iatbra@tiscalinet.it *Mon-Sat 0900-1900, Sun 0900-1500*. Just behind the Arena, Verona's tourist information centre is well placed but poor for browsing. As long as you know what you want, however, they'll probably be more than willing to help.

There's an 'office' at the railway station, which is no more than a man at a desk, but can nevertheless be useful for those arriving at the station. Porta Nuova FS, **T** 045 8000861, iatfs@tiscalinet.it *Mon-Sat 0900-1800, Sun 0900-1500*. It doesn't have information on trains themselves, but the train information office is next door.

There is also a small office at Verona (Villafranca) airport, **T** 045 8619163, iataeroporto@tiscalinet.it *Mon-Sat 0900-1800, Mon-Sat 0900-1800*.

Vicenza
piazza Matteotti 12, Vicenza, **T** 0444 320854, **F** 0444 994779, www.vicenzae.org *Mon-Sun 0900-1300, 1400-1800*. *Map 3, D6, p254* An office in piazza dei Signori is open 1000-1400, 1430-1830.

Brescia

piazza della Loggia 6, **T** 030 2400357,
www.comune.brescia.it *Winter Mon-Fri 0930-1230, 1400-1700,
summer Mon-Sat 0930-1830. Map 5, C2, p256*

Mantova

Azienda di Promozione Turistica, piazza Mantegna 6,
T 0376 328253, **F** 0376 363292, www.aptmantova.it *Mon-Sat
0830-1230, 1500-1800, Sun 0930-1230. Map 4, E6, p255*

Garda

Torri del Benaco, viale F Lavanda, **T/F** 045 7225120,
torriat@libero.it *Apr-Sep, Mon-Sat 1000-1300, 1600-1900.*

Malcesine, via Capitanato 6-8, **T** 045 7400044, **F** 045 7401633,
malcesine@aptgardaveneto.com *Summer Mon-Sat 0900-1300,
1600-1900, Sun 0900-1300, ring for winter hours.*

Torbole, via Lungolago Verona 19, **T** 0464 505177, **F** 0464
505643, info@gardatrentino.it *Easter-Nov, Mon-Sat 0900-1200,
1500-1830, mid-Jun-Sep Sun 1000-1200, 1600-1830, Dec-Easter
Mon-Fri 0900-1215, 1430-1815.*

Lessinia

Bosco Chiesanuova, piazza Chiesa 34, , **T/F** 045 7050088.
*Jul-Aug, Mon-Sun 0830-1245, 1500-1800, Sep-Jun closed Tue and
Sun, ring for opening hours.*

top are, from left to right, Hercules, Jupiter, Venus, Mercury, Apollo and Minerva. To its left is **Torre del Gardello**, also known as the *Torre delle Ore*, built in 1370 and the city's oldest bell tower. The clock is now bell-less, its ring having been taken to the Museo di Castelvecchio.

The column topped by a lion, symbol of Venice, is the **Colonna di San Marco**, first built in 1523. It was originally pulled down on the fall of the Venetian empire, but was re-erected with a new lion in 1886.

The **Fontana Madonna Verona**, one of the beloved symbols of the city, is in fact a mish-mash of Roman remains. The basin was taken from the thermal baths of Sant'Anastasia, the statue from the Capitol. The statue was erected in the 4th century in honour of the emperor's lifting of the city's debts. The fountain was added by Cansignorio della Scala in 1368.

On the eastern side of the piazza, the **Casa Mazzanti**, once used by the Scaligeri family for storing grain, has a cycle of allegorical frescoes by Cavalli from around 1530, illustrating ignorance, good government and envy. The portico, now filled with cafés selling various ice-cream concoctions, was built in 1480. In the cellars of these buildings, 3.5 m down from the present-day surface, the original paving of the Roman forum has been found. The houses opposite also have remnants of frescoes, from the 15th century, including a depiction of Hercules and the Hydra by Caroto.

Just to the south of the Casa Mazzanti, via della Costa leads under the **Arco della Costa** (Arch of the Rib) through to piazza dei Signori. The arch is so-called because of the whale bone which hangs underneath it. Various myths are attached to the bone, including one which states that the person upon whom it falls will

! Mastino I della Scala was murdered in the Volto Barbaro, between piazza Erbe and piazza dei Signori, in 1277. The following year, 166 heretics, whose capital punishment Mastino had commuted, were burnt at the stake in the Arena.

★ Bird's-eye view

The Torre dei Lamberti, one of many which once stood in the centre of Verona, rises high above piazza Erbe giving fantastic views of the city.

Grand designs
Surrounded by buildings built by and for the della Scala family, piazza dei Signori is Verona's most aristocratic space.

There is no world without Verona's walls
But purgatory, torture, hell itself.

Shakespeare, *Romeo and Juliet*, 1595

become king of Verona. The most probable theory about its origins is that it was hung there by one of the chemists whose shops were around the arch, perhaps as a sign, perhaps as a reminder of mortality, perhaps merely as decoration. The first depiction of the bone comes in a series of prints from 1743, though some believe it to have hung there long before this.

The so-called **Berlina** (pillory), where criminals would be put to be ridiculed) is in fact a 12th-century structure where the inauguration of the city's Podestà, or mayor, traditionally took place. Two lengths carved into the stone on the monument's southern side were the standards for the sale of fabric and other goods in the medieval market.

South of the Berlina, the shrine perched on top of a stone column, known as the **Colonna del Mercato**, is a copy. The figures are those of the Virgin Mary, St Peter, St Zeno and St Christopher. Erected in1401, the original is now in the Museo di Castelvecchio.

The newly restored **Domus Mercatorum**, on the corner of piazzetta XIV Novembre, was built in 1301, replacing a previous wooden structure. It was the headquarters for the trade and commerce authorities of the Comune. Behind here stood the tightly packed houses of the Jewish ghetto, demolished at the beginning of the 20th century ostensibly because it was considered unhealthy.

Opposite the Domus Mercatorum, the **Palazzo del Comune**, also known as the Palazzo della Ragione, was built in 1193, though the neo-classical façade by Giuseppe Barbieri was not added until 1810. The building, which encloses the cortile Mercato Vecchio (see p40), was the seat of power for the 12th-century Comune which ruled the city, and to this day, is still home to the city's magistrates. It was built around the slightly earlier **Torre dei Lamberti** (see p41), the tallest tower in the city, which now rises out of it.

Piazza dei Signori
Map 2, F6, p252

Known by Veronesi as *piazza Dante*, quiet piazza dei Signori is the noble opposite to piazza Erbe's proletarian style, a celebration not of commerce and the market, but of power and of poets, and in particular of the Scaligeri family, rulers of the city in the 13th and 14th centuries.

The piazza's most attractive building, and the best place from where to sit and watch the daily comings and goings, is the Renaissance **Loggia del Consiglio** (built between 1476 and 1492 by Fra' Giocondo) on the northwest side. With four elegant mullioned windows and frescoes above a loggia below, the building was built as a meeting place for the city's government. The statues along the top, supposed to be Veronesi from classical times are, from left to right, Vitruvius, Catullus, Pliny the Elder, Emilio Macro and Cornelius Nepos. It is now thought, however, that Catullus was probably the only one born near the city.

On the side of the **Palazzo del Comune** (see p37) which faces into piazza dei Signori are damaged coats of arms of Venetian governors and a stone face, through whose mouth people of the city were encouraged to post denouncements of their fellow citizens.

Also on this side of the piazza, both in the courtyard of the **Palazzo dei Tribunali** (the cortile del Tribunale, see p40) and between the two palaces, you can see through glass to some of the excavations of Roman remains below. The Palazzo dei Tribunali, complete with its tower, was first built as home to Cansignorio della Scala on top of what had already been a Scaligeri palace – that of Alberto della Scala. Later the building was headquarters of the Venetian rulers of the city, hence its other name, Palazzo del Capitano.

Dante's connection to the piazza is that he was a guest of the della Scala family in the **Palazzo Cangrande** (now the *Prefettura*)

Stairway to heaven

The Renaissance stairs in the cortile Mercato Vecchio, the Scala della Ragione, were once covered by a 15th-century loggia.

at the end of the piazza at the beginning of the 14th century. The portal is the work of influential 16th-century Veronese architect Sanmicheli. The building was heavily renovated in the 1930s, though the cool loggia is largely original. A plaque here announces the result of the 1866 plebiscite, which decided on the unification of Italy as a constitutional monarchy.

Ugo Zannoni's statue of **Dante** himself in the centre of the piazza is a relatively recent addition, added in 1865.

● *Members of the* Società Belle Arti Verona *exhibit in a few rooms off the southwest corner of the piazza in the Palazzo del Comune. Artists, who rotate every two weeks, tend to be rather conservative. The gallery space is open 1000-1200, 1600-1930 and is free.*

Cortile Mercato Vecchio
Map 2, G6, p253

Home to the famous **Scala della Ragione**, the cortile Mercato Vecchio is used on occasions for summer concerts and dance. The Renaissance Scala della Ragione, built between 1446 and 1452, also had a loggia construction above it until 19th-century 'restoration'.

★ Scavi Scaligeri/Centro Internazionale di Fotografia
cortile del Tribunale, piazza Viviani, **T** 045 8007490, www.comune.verona.it/scaviscaligeri *Opening times and prices change according to exhibitions. Map 2, F6, p252*

The mish-mash of ancient excavated remains under piazza Viviani and the cortile del Tribunale in the very centre of old Verona is the spectacular, if slightly damp, setting for excellent large-scale photography exhibitions. Recent exhibitions have included Fulvio Roiter and Sandro Santioli.

The excavations themselves include Roman sewers which were in use until the 20th century, Roman mosaics, graves from the

Middle Ages and façades from 5th-century houses. A paved Roman road runs directly under modern via Dante above.

★ Torre dei Lamberti
Cortile Mercato Vecchio, **T** 045 8032726. *Mon 1330-1930, Tue-Sun 0930-1930. €2.50 by lift, €1.50 on foot. Map 2, G5, p253*

Towering 83 m above the central piazzas of the city, the Torre dei Lamberti is one of the only remaining towers of around seventy that once traced the city skyline. Built partly for family prestige, partly for defence, these towers were found in many Italian cities. The octagonal Renaissance belfry at the top of the Torre dei Lamberti was added to the original 12th-century structure in 1464. 368 steps, or a lift, take you to the top, higher than any other building in the centre of the city, with wonderful views down to the piazzas and the rest of the city spread out below. The *Marangona* bell at the top was used as a fire alarm, while the *Rengo* bell announced council meetings in the Palazzo del Comune downstairs.

Arche Scaligeri
via Arche Scaligeri, **T** 045 8032726. *Map 2, F6, p252*

Inside a suitably ornate high wrought iron enclosure, the white Gothic tombs of the della Scala rulers of the city sit at the end of piazza dei Signori like enormous over-worked wedding cakes, topped with statues, each one more grandiosely decorative than the last. The fencing repeats the ladder motif which was the family's emblem (*scala* means ladder) and which can still be seen all over the city, emphasizing the hold the memory of the family still has over Verona. Outside the enclosed area is the most famous tomb of all, the **arca di Cangrande I**, from 1335 (Cangrande means 'Big Dog'). The equestrian statue is a copy, however, the original having been moved to the Museo di Castelvecchio

The Romeo and Juliet legend

Written between 1594 and 1596, Shakespeare's *Romeo and Juliet* is based firmly on a story which originated in folklore but was brought to prominence in various Italian 16th-century *novelle*. Elements of the story may go as far back as the *Ephesiaca* (by Xenophon of Ephesus, a 3rd-century Greek writer), in which the heroine takes what she believes is poison but which turns out to be sleeping potion and awakes in her tomb. By the time of Masuccio Salernitano's version, set in Siena and published in 1476, the heroine drinks potion to fake her death and sends a message to her lover which never reaches him. Luigi da Porto, in 1530, was the first to set events in Verona at the time of Bartolommeo della Scala. The idea that the story had origins in history seems to come from this time – it was set in a period of extreme inter-family hatred due to the Ghibelline and Guelf rivalries which split Italy, and Dante does mention both the Capelletti and Montecchi families together in a line in Purgatorio VI about dissent. The Capelletti family, however, were actually from Cremona. In da Porto's version the lovers are called Romeo and Giulietta, though he makes Juliet turn Romeo away from her balcony. Bandello further developed the story in 1554 and this was translated into French by Boaistuau in 1559. It seems that it was Arthur Brooke's translation of Boaistuau's version into English in 1562 with which Shakespeare was familiar. The extreme drama of the most famous version, is, however, mostly Shakespeare's, who shortened the time frame from several months to four or five days, tightened the structure of the storyline, deepened the atmosphere of surrounding tension, strengthened the characters, and wrote some of the English language's most famous lines into the bargain.

★ **Love letters**
The many layers of romantic graffiti surrounding the entrance to Juliet's house are an attraction in themselves, and one which does not seem to be discouraged.

(see p57) for safe-keeping. Next to it, the other equestrian statue is that on the **arca di Mastino II** (meaning 'Mastiff'), from 1350, and possibly sculpted by the same artist. The **arca di Cansignorio** ('Lord Dog'), dating from 1375, the most excessive of all, also has an equestrian statue and includes six guarding warriors.

● *Nearby, at 2-4 via Arche Scaligeri is the supposed **Casa di Romeo***. *The myth here has a slightly more historical basis in that a family by the name of Montecchi (Montague in Shakespeare's play) certainly lived here in the 14th century. The house is not open to the public though you can eat in the restaurant (see p138).*

Chiesa di Santa Maria Antica

via Arche Scaligeri, **T** 045 595508. *Mon-Sun 0730-1230, 1530-1900.*
Free. Map 2, F6, p252

A part of the Scaligeri complex of palaces and tombs, and with the
equestrian figure of Cangrande above its door, Santa Maria Antica
was the chapel of the Della Scala family. Romanesque in style, it
was rebuilt in the 12th century on top of an older Longobard
church. It is built with pale stone, punctuated by a few obligatory
red-brick stripes, and has a cream and pink marble floor onto
which light streams almost exclusively through a window above
the door, silhouetting Cangrande behind. Small, simple and serious
in format, with a nave and two aisles divided by columns, it is also
beautiful and atmospheric.

★ Casa di Giulietta

23 via Cappello, **T** 045 8034303. *Mon 1330-1930, Tue-Sun
0830-1930. Entrance to the house, €3.10, courtyard free.*
Map 2, G6, p253

An extraordinary indictment of modern tourism but also strangely
magnetic, Juliet's (supposed) house is, for the most part, a heaving
mass of day-trippers who throng in and out of the gates, stand
around in the courtyard taking photos of the famous balcony
(added to the building in the 1930s), fondle the right breast of the
statue of Juliet in the hope of better luck than she had, and troop
out again, leaving another layer of sentimental graffiti on the
multicoloured walls. All this is done without much of an apparent
sense of irony, or of the absurdity of it all. Perhaps it is this that
makes the place seem less cynical, less manipulative: the ridiculous
credulity of it all is somehow endearing.

Juliet, of course, was a fictional character (see box on the Romeo
and Juliet legend, p42). The Capulet family may similarly have
been made up – there are no records of a Capuleti family existing

in Verona at that time. So, at some point in the past, somebody decided that the Cappello family should stand in for them, and their house was made into a shrine to a fictional romance.

The inside of the house has been done up with commendable restraint and good taste. There are no cartoon postcards here, and surprisingly few people, the hordes seemingly happy for the most part to stay below and shout up at you when you step out onto the balcony. This adoration aside, it's worth a visit just to see the inside of a smart 14th-century townhouse faithfully recreated. There are fragments of frescoes by various painters including Veronese and Bernardino India, grand rooms, and costumes and the bed from Zeffirelli's 1968 film.

Porta dei Leoni
via Cappello. *Map 2, H7, p253*

Further down via Cappello from the Casa di Giulietta, the remains of one of the city's original (1st century AD) Roman gates have been added to, but the original form is still standing and clearly visible. At the southern edge of the Roman city, the gate had two large towers on either side. Sunk down into the road beside are excavations of other parts of the gateway, including the western tower.

★ Via Sottoriva
Map 2, E/F7, p252

One of the best preserved and most atmospheric of Verona's medieval streets, Sottoriva has a portico down one side and many 12th- and 13th-century buildings. Until changes that were made to the city after the 1882 flood, this was one of the places that was inundated most often. Right beside the river the street is at a low level (the name literally means *below the bank*). Once the busy and notorious home to fishermen, merchants, millers and *osterie*, the street lost some of its raison d'etre when the river level was lowered and the mills closed. However, it retained some of its best bars and restaurants, and it now has several of Verona's best nightspots, some good restaurants and some interesting shops and galleries.

Chiesa di Sant'Anastasia

piazza Sant'Anastasia, **T** 045 592813 *Mon-Sat 0930-1800, Sun 1300-1800. €2, €5 for combined ticket for five main churches. Map 2, D7, p252*

Verona's largest church is a vast and cavernous Gothic building. It contains the city's most reproduced work of art in Pisanello's 1438 weathered but magical fresco of St George and the Princess (entitled *San Giorgio e la principessa di Trebisonda*), albeit in an inaccessible position on the arch high above the Cappella Pellegrini to the right of the altar. Altichiero's fresco in the Cappella Cavalli is similarly impressive, and gives a good idea of how the city would have looked in the 1380s when it was painted, towards the end of the Scaligeri family dynasty. Built between 1290 and 1320 by Dominicans, the church is actually dedicated to a martyred Veronese Dominican friar, St Pietro, though the name has never stuck and the church is universally known by the name of a pre-existing church which stood on the same site. The campanile was not completed until 1434 and the upper part of the façade remains unfinished. The interior is composed of a nave and two aisles divided by enormous red marble pillars with Gothic capitals. The two holy water fonts at the back of the church are supported by marble statues of hunchbacks (*gobbi*). The one on the left as you enter was carved by Gabriele, father of the painter Veronese, in 1495. The second, in two-coloured marble, by Paolo Orefice, was added in 1591.

★ Galleria d'Arte Moderna

4 vicolo Volto Due Mori, corso Sant' Anastasia,
T 045 8001903. *Tue-Fri 0900-1900, Sat and Sun 0900-2000. Prices vary according to exhibitions. Map 2, E6, p252*

Verona's modern art museum is in the grand Palazzo Forti, a grand 13th-century building in which Napoleon once stayed. The old building has been sympathetically but strikingly converted into a modern gallery. The permanent collection on the ground floor includes some excellent international works as well as some local art of less obvious quality. Highlights include a great Spencer Tunick photo of nudes in New York (*9th Street and First Avenue – NYC 2*), Jane Phaff's energetic diptych *Fremdkörper*, Botto and Bruno's industrial photo montage *Red Sky* and a small bulbous Louise Bourgeois piece, *Fallen Woman*. Upstairs, a great exhibition space with high, occasionally patterned, ceilings is used for temporary exhibitions. In recent times these have included Kandinsky, Munch, Dadaism and Virginia Ferrari, a Verona-born sculptor, 12 of whose pieces were also placed in high-profile locations around the city.

Duomo, Sant'Elena and archeological excavations

piazza Duomo, **T** 045 592813. *Mon-Sat 0930-1800, Sun 1300-1800. €2, €5 for combined ticket for five main churches. Map 2, C5, p252*

Though sometimes overshadowed by the city's other spectacular churches, Verona's cathedral has a beautiful façade, a stunning Titian painting, a Sanmicheli-designed belltower, griffins and plenty of historical interest.

The building was initially designed by architect Nicolò in the 12th century, after the 1117 earthquake had destroyed the 8th-century cathedral. Despite subsequent Gothic alterations, it is Nicolò's features on and around the main double porch and canopy which remain particularly striking. An upper arch is supported by a lower

For whom the bells toll
Spiral stairs wrap around Torre dei Lamberti's bells, which once had important civic functions, such as calling people to meetings.

one, whose pillars rest on two marble griffins, their backs shiny from having been mounted by 860 years of Veronese children. Ornate and unusually descriptive stone reliefs around the door include the warriors Orlando (on the left) and Oliviero, better known as Roland and Oliver. The lunette above the door features a virgin and child, the annunciation to the shepherds and the adoration of the magi.

Equally striking are the stone sculptures over the side entrance: on one side Jonah is swallowed by a sea-monster, while on the other a dog bites a lion. These predate Nicolò's reconstructions.

Inside, Titian's *Assumption* in the Cappella Cartolari-Nichesola, the first on the left, is quite clearly the highlight. Poorly executed frescoes in the Cappella de Abazia-Lazzari next to it serve only to show just how good Titian's painting is. Framed by a columned altar by Sansovino, Titian's work is electric with human reaction. Titian aside, the most interesting works of art are Giovanni Maria Falconetto's 1503 paintings on four wooden panels in the Cappella Calcasol, illustrating the life of Christ.

Michele Sanmicheli's influence on the Duomo in the 16th century included designing the circular apse, the semicircular choir screen and the campanile. The latter, however, built on a 12th-century base, was not completed at the time – the top section was only added in 1913.

A door below the organ leads to the separate church of Sant'Elena, via a 12th-century loggia. Sant'Elena is uninspiring in itself, except that various parts of its floor are glass-covered, allowing views through to remains of a 4th-century Paleo-Christian structure, whose nave Sant'Elena more or less follows. When this first church was partially destroyed by fire at the end of the 6th century, it was replaced by a second basilica, mostly on the site of

! Two Gentlemen of Verona, the less famous of Shakespeare's two plays which feature the city, was his first romantic comedy. Many of its themes and techniques can be seen in later plays.

the present-day cloister. These Paleo-Christian structures were themselves built on pre-existing Roman remains, probably thermal baths and a temple to Minerva.

To reach the peaceful double-pillared cloisters of Sant'Elena you need to exit the Duomo and go around to the left of the front of the building.

While those in "inappropriate dress" will not be admitted, if you're lucky the ticket desk may have clothes to lend you to cover knees and shoulders, which seem to be the offending parts.

● *The **Biblioteca Capitolare** (piazza Duomo 13, **T** 045 596516, visits by appointment only) is a library holding various ancient and rare manuscripts. Founded in the 4th century, it was used by both Dante and Petrarch.*

Museo Canonicale
piazza Duomo, **T** 045 592813. *Sat 1000-1300, Sun 1430-1800, closed Mon-Fri.* €2. *Map 2, C5, p252*

In rooms off the cloisters of Sant'Elena (see above), the Museo Canonicale contains a collection once largely in the custody of various churches around the city – many of which no longer exist – but now in the possession of the Duomo. The Renaissance room is the most interesting, with paintings by Morone, Caroto and Giolfino among others. Downstairs there are some Roman artefacts, mostly fragments, but including a beautiful glass engraved with figures.

Museo Miniscalchi-Erizzo
via Santo Mamaso 2/a, **T** 045 8032484. *Tue-Fri 1600-1900, Sat-Sun 1030-1200, 1600-1900.* €5. *Map 2, E4, p252*

In the beautiful 15th-century Palazzo Miniscalchi, with faded frescoes and elaborate Gothic arched windows, is an odd collection of antique furniture, Renaissance drawings, Roman glassware and a 19th-century reconstruction of a 16th-century suit of armour. In the grand *Sala della Bifone*, with an impressive 18th-century inlaid wooden box, sunlight streams in through the windows at the front of the house. The highlight, however, is probably the drawings, notably those by Brusasorci, Veronese and Guido Reni.

Corso Porta Borsari and Porta Borsari
Map 2, H3, p253

Following the route of the Roman *decumanus maximus* west from piazza Erbe, corso Porta Borsari is one of Verona's most attractive streets and ends with one of its most impressive Roman remains, the remarkably intact gateway of Porta Borsari. Lined with shops and cafés, which tend to be less smart and have a little more character than those on via Mazzini, its prime rival for top shopping street, corso Porta Borsari is also more used by Veronesi. Halfway along on the northern side is the small Romanesque church of **San Giovanni in Foro**, with a newly-restored façade.

Porta Borsari itself is a three-tiered structure of arches, built in the 1st century AD as the monumental entrance to the city on the east-west Postumian way, and thus the most important. The design was much admired in the Renaissance, and motifs were borrowed by architects such as Sanmicheli. Originally the gate would have been a three-dimensional building – all that remains today is the western façade. The name, almost certainly a medieval invention, comes from the word *bursarii*, meaning those who collected taxes at the gates. The original Roman name was *Porta di Giove*, Gate of Jupiter.

Via Mazzini
Map 2, I4-G6, p253

Via Mazzini, now probably Verona's most famous street, and certainly its richest, was once dirty and unpaved, unimportant and unloved. Only with the creation and subsequent rise in importance of piazza Bra from the 16th century onwards did the street begin to take on something of its current aspect.

Nowadays it is one of Italy's smartest shopping streets, packed with people strolling up and down its shiny marble length from piazza Erbe at one end to piazza Bra at the other. It has also become something of a stage for the selling of fake handbags and black market CDs, and teams of men offering tourists the chance to "find the coin" in order to double their money. These activities have not gone down well with shopkeepers on via Mazzini, who feel the tone of their street is being lowered and have threatened to shut up their shops in protest.

South of the centro storico

At the other end of via Mazzini from the enormous spread of piazza Erbe, piazza Bra forms an alternative centrepiece to the city, with the huge amphitheatre of the Arena dominating it. To the west, Castelvecchio has all the attributes you'd wish for in a castle, plus a great bridge and an interesting museum. Further west, San Zeno is justifiably the city's favourite church, but to the south there is much less of interest. As the roads widen and become more modern towards the station, the city loses its antique feel, and, though there are occasional points of interest such as Juliet's supposed tomb, the city becomes rather plain.

▸▸ *See Sleeping p118, Eating and drinking p143, Bars and clubs p168*

▸▸ *See Sleeping p118, Eating and drinking p143, Bars and clubs p168*

◉ Sights

Piazza Bra
Map 2, J3, p253

The name 'Bra' is a shortening of the Lombard *braida*, meaning widening. Outisde of the original Roman city walls, the piazza was not considered a piazza at all until Sanmicheli's building of the Palazzo degli Honori in the 16th century. It wasn't until the *Listone* (the wide marble-paved promenade) was paved in 1782 that piazza Bra became the most popular spot for the *passegiata*, the evening stroll.

These days it is a sprawling hub of the city, a strange irregular shape, bordered (and dominated) by the Arena on one side, the smart buildings and cafés along the *Listone* on another, a well preserved stretch of the 13th-century Scaligeri walls and the Gran Guardia on another, and finally the 19th-century neo-classical Palazzo Barbieri. The space these disparate elements enclose has at its centre an area of trees and an ugly modern fountain.

The double arch gates of **Portoni Bra**, complete with a clock, which lead south from the piazza onto corso Porta Nuova, through which many modern travellers enter the old city, were built in 1480 by the Viscontis, primarily to carry a walkway from Castelvecchio along the top of the *mura comunali* (communal wall) to the Visconti citadel to the southeast of piazza Bra. From here, keeping to the left side of the square, the **Listone** is a wide pavement polished by centuries of strolling feet. Its buildings, behind the rather touristy cafés which line this side of the square, are piazza Bra's most attractive. Most famous is number 18, the sturdy Palazzo degli Honori, built by Sanmicheli in 1555. Garibaldi addressed the Veronese people from the balcony here, in 1867. The **Gran Guardia**, next to the Portoni Bra, was designed by Domenico Curtoni, Sanmicheli's nephew, in 1610, but work was suspended in 1614 and the building was not completed until 1821. The ostentatiously grandiose **Palazzo Barbieri** (also known as the Gran Guardia Nuova) was built between 1836 and 1848 to Corinthian-style designs by Giuseppe Barbieri and is now used as the city hall. After damage in the Second World War, the semicircular appendage was added behind.

★ Arena

piazza Bra, **T** 045 8003204, www.arena.it *Mon 1330-1930, Tue-Sun 0830-1930, 0900-1530 during opera season. €3.10, €1 on the first Sun of the month. Map 2, I/J4, p253 See also Opera, p176*

Verona's most famous sight is its giant elliptical Roman amphitheatre, the third largest still in existence after the Colisseum in Rome and the little-visited amphitheatre in Capua. Still dominating much of the city, it is used as a 20,000-seater stadium and a theatre for the summer opera season. In Roman times it may have held even more – up to 30,000 are thought to have watched gladiatorial combat and animal fights here after it was built in the 1st century AD. The *ala*, or wing, near to the beginning of via Mazzini, is all that remains of the outer ring of the amphitheatre, most of which was destroyed in the 1183 earthquake. Originally this outer ring was 152 m across at the widest part. The surviving inner ring has 72 pairs of arches, one above the other. Inside there are 44 rows of seats with 64 *vomitoria*, the entrances onto the seats from the long ambulatories, the passageways inside the structure.

Until Gallienus incorporated the Arena into his extended city defences in 285 AD, the Arena stood outside the city walls. In the Middle Ages shops were built into the arches and it became a haunt of prostitutes. It also seems to have constantly remained a source of pride for the people of the city, however, and though it has at times been used as a source of stone, it has also been patched up through the ages, and it remains remarkably intact. In 1913 Verdi's Aida was performed in the Arena, and it has been the setting for the famous summer opera season ever since.

Apart from its sheer size and extraordinary antiquity, the most startling aspect of the Arena is how similar to modern stadiums it is. Although it's hard to beat watching an opera here, there's also something to be said for visiting in midwinter, when, without stages and lighting rigs, the stark scale of the place is easier to appreciate.

● *Behind the Arena, in a small area called piazza Mura di Gallieno, is one of the few remaining pieces of the city walls constructed in a hurry by the Roman emperor in 258 AD. Despite houses being built into them, the haphazard nature of their construction is still obvious.*

Museo Lapidario Maffeiano

piazza Bra 28, **T** 045 8003204. *Mon 1330-1930, Tue-Sun 0830-1400. €2.10. On the right just to the south of the Portoni Bra, off the southwestern corner of piazza Bra. Map 2, J2, p253*

Scipione Maffei, 1675-1755, was one of the great collectors of Greek and Roman inscriptions and stone carvings. His set of 600 fragments still makes up one of the world's most important collections of ancient text. The first floor has around 100 Greek inscriptions and sculptures, some very well preserved, especially the sepulchre of a woman (number 43), complete with an angel playing an instrument. Also striking is number 77, a carving of two young men – Pamphilos and Alexandros – with horses, and two symbolic snakes wrapped around the trees. A terrace on this floor also gives great views over piazza Bra. The second floor has some wonderfully detailed sarcophagi, and some Etruscan urns in terracotta, some still coloured. The courtyard outside, which you can visit, is filled with pieces of Roman columns and carvings, some looking implausibly new. Three large sides of a tomb here came from a 2nd-century Veronese temple to Bacchus.

San Fermo Maggiore and Inferiore

stradone San Fermo, **T** 045 8007287. *Mon-Sat 0930-1800, Sun 1300-1800. €2, €5 for combined ticket for five main churches. Map 2, I7, p253*

East of piazza Bra, by Ponte Navi, the church of San Fermo is a complicated, red-and-white striped mix of Romanesque and Gothic styles. The stripes, characteristic of Veronese Romanesque architecture, are made up of alternating brick and tufa. The 24 bronze door panels are a recent addition, made by Luciano Minguzzi in 1997. The structure is actually made up of two churches, one piled on the other. The dark atmospheric San Fermo Inferiore was built between 1065 and 1143, the towering San Fermo Maggiore added from 1261 to 1332. The interior of the upper church has a vast and ornate wooden ribbed vault ceiling which gives the impression of being inside the hull of an enormous upturned boat. Panels in the ceiling are decorated with 416 portraits of saints. All of these are reproduced on a panel along a wall of the nave. Other highlights include Pisanello's mournful frescoes around the Brenzoni mausoleum to the left of the entrance, and fantastical frescoes on the vaults of the apse and on its surrounding triumphal arch, the latter attributed to Lorenzo Veneziano. Ruskin wrote of the beautiful façade that it was "chiselled and fitted with exquisite precision, all Venetian work being coarse in comparison".

The **Chiostro Francescano** (cloister), which you pass on your way down to the lower church, can be viewed through a barred window, but is not open to the public. It is dotted with various headless statues. **San Fermo Inferiore** is a cool, atmospheric Romanesque space, with fragmented 12th- and 14th-century frescoes and heavy stone pillars between three aisles. Some of the flagstones have been lifted to reveal the foundations of an even older 5th-century Paleo-Christian structure.

Castelvecchio

corso Castelvecchio 2, **T** 045 592985, **F** 045 8010729, www.comune.verona.it/castelvecchio/cvsito *Mon 1330-1930, Tue-Sun 0830-1930, ticket office closes at 1845. €3.10, free first Sun of month. For guided tours* **T** *045 8000466,* **F** *045 8000804. Bookshop Mon 1330-1800, Tue-Sun 0830-1800. Art library Mon-Fri 0900-1800, Sat 0900-1400. Map 2, I1, p253*

Now the Civic Museum of Art, Cangrande II della Scala built the Castelvecchio as Castello San Martino in Aquaro between 1354 and 1356, more to protect himself from the Veronese population than because of any fear of outsiders. The castle was renamed Castelvecchio ('old castle') by the Milanese Visconti when they built Castel San Pietro and Castel San Felice. The wing alongside the river was built by Napoleonic forces at the beginning of the 19th century. Previously this side of the parade ground was open to the water.

The castle continued to be used as a military site until 1921, when it was chosen as the site for the city's civic art collection. Carlo Scarpa's influential and respected 1958-1964 restoration completed the transition into a modern exhibition space. Scarpa's cleverness was in stripping out previous refurbishments and making his conversion obviously modern, so that it sits *with* the bare structure of the castle rather than trying to be a part of it.

The ground floor is set aside for sculpture and objects found in and around Verona. The first room has stone reliefs from the early medieval and Romanesque periods as well as Longobard jewellery, coins, spoons and a silver plate. The relief of Christ between St Peter and St Paul, taken from the Duomo, was sculpted by Peregrinus in the 1120s. He is credited with being the first to introduce the Romanesque style to the city. In the centre of the room, and centre of attention, is the sarcophagus of martyred saints, Sergius and Bacchus. Around the stone sides the story of their downfall is told in some detail, Bacchus eventually being clubbed to death and Sergius decapitated. On the lid two archers shoot at an eagle.

In **Room 2**, two beautiful statues of St Catherine and St Cecilia are the enigmatic highlights, though St John the Baptist also has a certain wooden charm. All three of these are from the first half of the 14th century and were taken from Sant'Anastasia.

After another two rooms of religious statuary, a 14th-century tomb slab bears the inscription "Why are you so proud, gentlemen?

Why such blindness? What I am now you will be and you cannot avoid it. Give what you have while it is still yours; after death it is yours no longer. Youth passes like a flower and the wind."

Outside the sculpture gallery, the large bell is from Torre del Gardello, at the end of piazza Erbe. On one side is a depiction of San Zeno fishing, while on the other, a crowned, winged dog up a ladder is the symbol of Cangrande della Scala.

Following the trail of rooms up through the dungeons into the palace area of the castle, a painting of the *Madonna Enthroned with Child* in **Room 7** begins to show some Giotto-esque evolution towards the Renaissance, away from the stark primitivism of the stoned-looking *Madonna del Latte* opposite. Also here is the sword of Cangrande, taken from his tomb in 1921 to mark the sixth centenary of Dante's death.

Room 8 contains three *sinopie*, or preparatory drawings, which were uncovered when the Circle of Altichiero (also here) was removed from San Zeno. For whatever reason, only the composition of the third was accepted.

Room 10, the Pisanello room, is highly frescoed with original della Scala symbols and patterns. Pisanello, who trained in the city, was almost certainly responsible for the strikingly beautiful *Madonna of the Quail*, seeming to be a precursor of much later painters such as Klimt with its magical and ornate qualities. Jacopo Bellini is also represented here, as is Pannonio, whose Madonna's pearls glisten especially effectively.

The city's collection of Flemish paintings is kept in **Room 11**. Here Van Cleef's *Interior with Kitchen* is wonderfully busy and bawdy, while Leyden's *Crucifixion* is colourful yet atmospherically twisted and pained.

Giovanni Bellini's stark *Crucifixion* dominates the large **Hall of the Reggia**, though two of his paintings in Room 13, upstairs, both depictions of the *Madonna and Child*, outshine it.

Rooms 14-16 concentrate on three Veronese painters, Francesco Morone, Francesco Bonsignori, and Liberale. None of

★ **Works of art**

Best

• Equestrian Monument of Cangrande I della Scala,
  Castelvecchio, p57.
• Mantegna's *Maestà della Vergine*, San Zeno, p63.
• Pisanello's *St George and the Princess*, Sant'Anastasia, p46.
• Spencer Tunick's *9th Street and First Avenue – NYC 2*, Galleria
  d'Arte moderna, p47.
• Titian's *Assumption*, Duomo, p47.

these, however, quite manage the Renaissance subtlety of
expression or dynamics of composition of Andrea Mantegna's *Holy
Family with a Female Saint* in **Room 17**. In **Room 18**, Giolfino's
Stories of St Agatha is primitive, but notable for its depiction of
15th-century piazza dei Signori.

Through a small section of weaponry you come out to Verona's
most famous sculpture, the striking *Equestrian Monument of
Cangrande I della Scala*, the most successful of the Scaligeri leaders
of the city. Taken from his tomb (where a copy now stands, see
p41), it would originally have been painted. In the 17th century the
statue was knocked off its plinth by a bolt of lightning. It was
moved here in 1911. Sitting back in his saddle, Cangrande surveys
the world with a broad but enigmatic smile. Its sculptor, though
clearly exceptionally talented, remains unknown. The same hands
are, however, also thought to be responsible for the similar,
though comparatively lifeless, statue of Mastino II, currently at the
foot of the stairs to the Sala Boggian, the temporary exhibition
space in the corner of the castle.

In **Room 20**, Morando's ambitious and colourful 16th-century
altarpiece is a virtuoso Renaissance work of art, as are his four
saints in the same room. He is outdone, however, for vitality,
humour and humanity by Gianfrancesco Caroto's small *Portrait of a
Child with a Drawing*.

In **Room 21**, Caroto's brother Giovanni's self-portrait with his wife, Placida, is a fragment of an altarpiece destroyed by fire, but still retains enormous power and serenity, as does an enigmatic *Portrait of a Monk* by Moretto in the same room.

Tintoretto (1518-1594) and Veronese (1528-1588) are probably the two best known of the city's painters, though both did some of their best work in Venice. Both are represented in **Room 22**.

Amongst the Mannerists in **Room 23**, Palma il Giovane's *Imploring for the Cessation of the Plague in Verona* is the strongest, while in **Room 24**, the city's 17th-century taste for the dark, chiaroscuro figures of Caravaggio is demonstrated in Basetti's *Portrait of an Old Man with a Book* and Bernardi's *Holy Family*. The 17th-century continues in similarly dramatic form in **Room 25** with Strozzi's *Expulsion From Eden*. Ridolfi's two canvases of the *Annunciation from the church of Santa Croce* are beautiful but oddly different in style, the Virgin baroque, the angel more Venetian in character.

In the final room, **Room 26**, Giordano's Cupid lifts Ariadne's blue cloak to show her nude body to Bacchus, while Theseus sails away into the distance on the right.

Ponte di Castelvecchio
Map 2, I1, p253

Built at the same time as the Castle, in the mid-14th century, Castelvecchio's bridge (also known as Ponte Scaligeri) was an escape route, away from the city towards the friendly north. The bridge was only made accessible from the city in 1870, after the unification of Italy, when an opening was made in the castle wall and a ramp built across the Collegio courtyard. Of the bridge's three spans, the one nearest the castle is larger than the others. This was to allow trading boats to pass through. Like Ponte Pietra downstream, the Castelvecchio bridge was reconstructed after it was blown up by the fleeing Germans at the end World War II.

Arco dei Gavi
Map 2, I2, p253

Beside Castelvecchio, this Roman triumphal arch, designed by
Vetruvius, once stood on the via Postumia, to the south of the city
walls. The paving stones beneath are also Roman, as are the cart ruts
worn into them. The arch was built in the first century AD to honour
the local Gavia family, whose statues would have stood in the niches
now facing the river. It was reconstructed in its present position in
1932. Beyond, the piazza Castelvecchio has good views of the river.

Chiesa San Lorenzo
corso Cavour, **T** 045 592813. *Mon-Sat 0930-1800, Sun 1300-1800.*
€2, €5 for combined ticket for five main churches. Map 2, H3, p253

Halfway between Porta Borsari and Castelvecchio, San Lorenzo has
possibly the city's most beautiful interior. A simple, uncluttered and
largely unaltered 12th-century Romanesque space, the cool nave
and two aisles are separated by alternate marble columns and
striped brick and tufa pillars. Arches support a *matroneo* or women's
gallery with more arches which runs around three sides of the
church above the aisles. The whole place is perfectly proportioned,
and the stone and brick walls add a sense of style. Fragments of
frescoes are from the 12th and 15th centuries. Above the altar is
Domenico Brusasorci's 1566 Virgin and Child with Saints John,
Lorenzo and Agustino. The façade, which can be seen by exiting
through a door at the back of the church, is 'bookended' between
two stone towers. The marble porch above the side entrance was
added in the 15th century. Pieces of columns in the courtyard
outside are from an earlier 8th-century church on the same site.
   ● *Palazzo Bevilacqua, opposite San Lorenzo on corso Cavour, was
designed by Michele Sanmicheli in 1530 and is considered a
Renaissance masterpiece. Architectural details such as the spiral fluting
on the first floor, are borrowed from Porta Borsari along the road.*

Basilica San Zeno

piazza San Zeno, **T** 045 592813. *Mon-Sat 0830-1800, 1300-1800.*
€2, €5 for combined ticket for five main churches. Map 1, D2, p250

Verona's most famous and most popular church is also its most
spectacular. An enormous, pale, weather-beaten, sun-bleached yet
elegant building, it dominates the southwest corner of the city.
Inside it is a majestic space, with characteristic Veronese
Romanesque stripes of stone and brick, pink marble columns, an
impressive 'keel' wooden ceiling and faded pastel tones shining in
the sunlight which streams in.

Zeno himself arrived in the city from Northern Africa in the 4th
century AD and is surrounded by legend. He was ordained bishop
of Verona in 362 and was a keen fisherman – there is much
iconography around the city of him with a fish on the end of a line.

Facing San Zeno from its piazza in front of the church, the
13th-century Benedictine tower to the left (all that remains of the
monastery that once stood there) acts as a sturdy counterpoint to
the basilica's ornate beauty. The monastery was originally built here
in the 9th century, together with a church on the site of an existing
Paleo-Christian chapel. King Pepin consecrated the site in 806. In
963, after damage inflicted on it by the invading Hungarians,
rebuilding was done, and a new church consecrated. 11th-century
work to extend the building to its current size was set back by
extensive damage in the 1117 earthquake, whereupon the current
design was implemented between 1120 and 1138. The great rose
window, known as the *Ruota della Fortuna* (Wheel of Fortune), with
its figures rising and falling, was added by Brioloto around 1200.

To the right of the façade, the 62 m-belltower rises unattached to
the main building, emphasizing its height. Built between 1045 and
the middle of the 12th century, it also has the characteristic stripes of
red brick and creamy volcanic tufa stone, as well as a conical roof.

On the façade itself, the work of Nicolò is recognisable from
his portal to the Duomo, with a porch resting on two columns,

Religious devotion
San Zeno is held in special affection by the people of the city, and its elegant cloisters demonstrate the care with which the church is still looked after.

which in turn sit on two lions. The bas-relief scenes to the right of the porch are also his, including stories from the Old Testament and the legend of King Theodoric hunting a deer on horseback and being led down into hell. Theodoric, though his influence on the city was largely positive, was never forgiven for destroying a church. One of Nicolò's collaborators, Guglielmo, is responsible for the largely New Testament scenes on the other side. The bas-relief in the lunette above the doors retains some of its original colouration, protected as it is from the elements by the porch above. It depicts San Zeno converting the city to Christianity. The famous brass doors of the church are now only viewable from the inside.

The entrance to the church is through a gate into the cloister between the monastery and the façade. The cloister itself is a beautiful space. Arched with double columns, similar to those in the Duomo's cloister, there is a loggia on the north side which originally housed a fountain for ablutions.

From the cloister you enter the church through a side door, coming into a large, light-filled space with a central nave and two aisles divided by alternate pillars and columns. At the front of the church, steps on either side rise to a raised presbytery, while steps in the centre go down to the crypt below, inaccessible, but with St Zeno's tomb visible at its end. Frescoes, notably those either side of the presbytery, show the first signs of Giotto's influence on the city's art, and an evolution of style away from the medieval towards the Renaissance.

Faces in some of these works, such as St George killing the dragon and surrounding scenes on the right, begin to look more human and there is some limited use of perspective, shadow, and three-dimensional space. These same frecoes also show a particularly ancient taste for graffiti – some of the scratched inscriptions, in Latin, go back to as early as 1390. Opposite St George, among more frescoes on the other wall, the *Crucifixion* is attributed to Altichiero.

Mantegna's 1457-59 triptych altarpiece, *Maestà della Vergine* (Madonna, Angels and Saints), takes the first tentative steps seen in San Zeno's frescoes to a whole new level to create a celebrated Renaissance masterpiece. The painting is important for some of its stylistic innovations: the space seems to extend across the three panels and back into the distance. An ancient pillared structure behind the figures is used to create a sense of depth, accentuated by a hanging decoration painted across the front to create foreground, and clouds behind. The composition of figures follows the perspective of this structure back into the painting. Furthermore, the figure reading, on the far right, faces diagonally out of the picture, another Renaissance ploy to enhance the sense of space and depth.

The 14th-century frescoes on the triumphal arch above Mantegna's masterpiece, attributed to Martino da Verona, also play with architecture and perspective.

At the other end of the church, the 48 brass panels of the 12th-century doors are now badly lit and hard to see. They are illustrated with Biblical scenes and stories from the life of San Zeno. Those on the left door (on the right as you look from inside the church) are older, predating the 1117 earthquake. Many have great narrative force and are both impressively intricate and visually striking.

Francesco Turbido's altarpiece at this end of the church, to the left of the doors, is another fine Renaissance work: a busy composition of the Madonna and Child with three other saints, one of which is San Zeno.

San Bernardino and Chiostro Sant'Antonio
strada A Provolo 28. *Jun-Sep 0800-1230, 1500-1930, Oct-May, 0800-1230, 1500-2000. Free. Map 1, E3, p250*

While the church itself is fairly unremarkable, San Bernardino's cloister, the **Chiostro Sant'Antonio**, is an attractive, open, quiet place with birdsong, striking wrought-iron gates, daisies, flaking paint, ancient graffiti, frescoes and tombstones. The highlight, however is the ex-library of the monastery, the beautifully frescoed **Sala Morone**, which you may have to ask to see.

Lido di Verona
via Galliano, **T** 045 8103529, **F** 045 8199449. *Jun-mid-Sep, Mon-Sun 0930-2030. €5.50 all day, €3.90 half day, kids (13 and under) €3.30/€2.90. Five minutes walk west from Porta Palio. Map 1, E1, p250*

Verona's municipal swimming pool is spectacular. There are four super-clean pools: two junior and two olympic-size, one of which has lanes. There is a big grassy area, there are free sun loungers, a free cloakroom and the 16th-century city walls rise up one side of the complex. Swimming caps are obligatory but can be bought on-site for €3.

Tomba di Giulietta and the Museo degli Affreschi
via del Pontiere 35, **T** 045 8000361 *Mon 1345-1930, Tue-Sun 0830-1930. €2.60, free first Sun of month. Map 1, F6, p250*

Set in a former Capuchin monastery, the supposed site of Juliet's tomb (and therefore also of her and Romeo's deaths) is surprisingly evocative, especially if you can manage to visit outside peak times when the cold, damp and quiet of the dark sunken chamber are allowed to predominate. The fact that this was certainly somebody's tomb adds to the ability to suspend disbelief, at least for a moment. In the tomb chambers themselves there is none of the kitsch which prevails in Juliet's house (see p44). The only object of dubious taste here is an *Albero dei Desideri*, a wishing tree, beside the pergola entrance to the museum. It is covered by various wishes of members of the public on scraps of paper or postcards, many wishing for Romeo and Juliet-related romance, but with happier endings, presumably.

The Fresco Museum tends to be overlooked, or at least rushed through, by those wishing to visit the tomb, and suffers a degree of credibility loss because of its permanent juxtaposition with the cult of a fictional character. This is a shame, as the museum contains some of the city's best Renaissance works, though many are badly damaged.

Verona was once known as the 'painted city' (*urbs picta*), so numerous were its frescoes, many from the Renaissance. Many were brought here when their life as frescoes, exposed to the elements was already coming to an end. Others were salvaged from the riverfront palazzi which were demolished after the 1882 floods. The museum starts on the first floor with some of the latter examples, including Bernardino India and Domenico Brusasorci's 16th-century frescoes from the Palazzo di Fionio della Seta, once considered one of the city's most beautiful buildings. Most of the other great Veronese Renaissance painters are also represented here: Del Moro, Torbido, Altichiero, Morone and Farinati. Del Moro's *Child with a Dog* is tantalisingly the only remaining fragment of the frescoes which once decorated the façade of the Bevilacqua-Lazise palace.

Going further back in time, one room has the rare multi-layered medieval frescoes from the shrine of St Nazaro and St Celso, some dated as far back as 996, though most are 12th-century. The style is radically different from those of the Renaissance, with strong lines and primitive figures.

The highlight of the museum is the recreation of the room in the Palazzo Guarienti which held Paolo Farinati's mythological frescoes. Though the fireplace and the windows are not originals, the room is laid out exactly as it was, and is the perfect way to view Farinati's Renaissance masterpieces (plastic fig trees notwithstanding). The three graces on the end wall are particularly well executed as are the women playing instruments in the corners of the room. Other featured characters include Mercury, Venus and Diana.

Downstairs in the 17th-century church of San Francesco, the highlights among a collection of paintings are Venetian Girolamo Bonsignori's *Annunciation*, with delicate botanical detail, Gianfrancesco Caroto's desperately sad *Three Archangels* and Antonio Palma's richly detailed *Adoration of the Magi*.

In the basement there is a collection of Roman *amphorae* – bottles which would have been used for transporting and storing oil, food and wine.

Museo della Radio d'Epoca

c/o ITIS Gallileo Ferraris, via del Pontiere 40, **T** 045 505855. *Mon-Fri 1400-1730 but also most mornings from 0800-1200. Free. Map 1, F5, p250*

You might not expect a museum of antique radios to be very exciting, and the fact that it was inside a technical institute might not inspire you either. However, although the setting is very plain, the radios themselves are a revelation – from finely carved art deco pieces to mammoth juke-box like machines to small portable Bakelite gems, they are, mostly, beautiful objets d'art, and a fine contrast to Juliet's tomb opposite.

Fiera

viale del lavoro 8, **T** 045 8298111, **F** 045 8298288, www.veronafiere.it Tickets, **T** 045 8298170 *Map 1, J3, p251 See also events, p187*

Verona's trade fair, to the south of the old city in the industrial zone, is known primarily for hosting *Vinitaly*, Italy's biggest wine fair, in April, but also has fairs covering everything from minerals to nautical equipment, agriculture to buses. Tickets are available from the veronafiere website or by phone, though many fairs have restrictions on the numbers of non-trade visitors. Special buses run from the centre of the city during large fairs.

North and east of the Adige

*The sprawling narrow streets of Verona's left bank are known as
Veronetta. This is the area that was controlled by Austria after the
city was divided in 1801. It was also the area worst affected by the
floods of 1882, which destroyed many of its houses and mills and
prompted the filling in of the branch of the river – now
commemorated in street names such as piazza Isolo and Interrato
dell'Acqua Morta. From San Giorgio in Braida in the north to the
Cimitero Monumentale in the south, the area is a lively maze of
streets with some of the city's best small bars and* trattorie. *Mainly
residential, it has noticeably fewer tourists than the* centro storico
*on the right bank, but a few excellent sights, the city's university and
plenty of atmosphere. Behind Veronetta rises the hill of San Pietro,
probably the original site of Veronese inhabitation with the Teatro
Romano and Castello San Pietro. Behind this are the city walls,
beyond which the Colline Veronese rise slowly towards the Alps,
with olive groves, villas and vines.*

▸▸ *See Sleeping p126, Eating and drinking p149, Bars and clubs p169*

Sights

Teatro Romano and the Museo Archeologico

Rigaste Redentore 2, **T** 045 8000360. *Mon 1330-1930, Tue-Sun
0830-1930. Ticket office closes at 1845. €2.60, free first Sun of month.
For information on summer music, dance and theatre events*
T *045 8077201, www.estateteatraleveronese.it Map 2, C8, p252
See also Music, p180*

Rising all the way up the hill of San Pietro from the river to the
temple at its peak and stretching from Ponte Pietra to Ponte
Postumia (which no longer exists), Verona's Roman theatre was
the grandest in northern Italy, on completion around the end of

the first century BC. Only fragments of its former glory remain today, uncovered from some of the buildings that were constructed on top of it, and partially reconstructed in places after damage by earthquakes and plundering for stone. There is, however, enough to suggest its former greatness, and enough to make it a popular and viable contemporary performance space for a summer season of theatre and music.

The original stage was a three-storey structure running along the riverbank. Behind this, the main semicircular seating area, supported by radial walls, had a diameter of 105 m. Much of this survives, as do some of the radial walls, especially on the southern side of the site where the original structure can easily be seen. Behind this would have been galleries and then three man-made terraces with loggias. The third terrace was the top of the hill, where a temple stood on the current site of Castel San Pietro. The whole structure was over 40 m high. The terraces still exist and are incorporated into the Museo Archeologico.

Much of the credit for the excavations which unearthed the theatre is given to Andrea Manga, whose statue sits among fragments of Roman columns to the north of the seating area. However, enough of the theatre was there in the 16th century for Palladio to make exquisitely detailed architectural drawings of how the theatre must have once looked, reproductions of which are in the Museo Archeologico, together with an architectural model based on his designs.

Near Manga's statue is a plaque commemorating the first production of Romeo and Juliet in the theatre in the summer of 1948, since when a regular season of theatre, music and dance has taken place.

The city's **Museo Archeologico** is spread through the upper part of the theatre, including the former monastery of San

! In the flood of 1882 the level of the Adige rose to a height of 12 m. Two-thirds of the city were flooded.

Best seats in the house
*The curved Roman seats of the Teatro Romano, like those of the
Arena, are still well-used by modern-day theatre-goers.*

Girolamo. The first room has a mosaic of Bacchus with a panther at his feet, and the openings of Roman drains designed to take water away from the theatre. The beautiful 15th- to 16th-century Chiostro dei Gesuati here is home to a varied collection of Roman fragments of funerary monuments and mosaics. Among the most interesting is a cippus (a small column marking a significant place, often a burial site) with a naked eros looking rather sad and leaning on an upturned torch, a symbol of dying. Opposite, on the right as you enter the cloister, is a cylindrical funeral urn topped by a rabbit clasped in the claws of a lion. The convent cells have some pre-Roman finds, including bronze Etruscan devotional offerings from the 6th century BC. Also here is a beautiful female bronze two-faced Roman bust. A large collection of headless Roman statues and body-less Roman heads is less interesting. The Grande Terrazza has a mixture of more funeral monuments and fragments of columns as well as some good views. The most beautiful part of all, the tree-lined *Seconda Passegiata*, one of the original terraces of the theatre, with stunning views over the city, is only open at weekends and on holidays.

Castel San Pietro
Map 2, B8, p252

The probable site of the first settlement in the city, then of the Roman Temple which later crowned the hill and later still of the

Visconti castle, is now a largely abandoned 19th-century Austrian-built barracks. Plans have been mooted to use the building as exhibition space for some of the city's museums, but as yet there is no sign of action. It is, nevertheless, one of the city's most visited attractions, especially at sunset, when lovers stroll up here in order to gaze back down over the city below. The views are spectacular, and even the walk up is pleasant, steps winding up the hillside between houses with occasional glimpses of the Roman theatre to the right.

Chiesa San Giovanni in Valle
via San Giovanni in Valle. *Mon-Fri 0900-1130, 1700-1830.*
Map 1, C7, p250

A combination of white doves, cacti and some eccentric internal decoration give this the feel of a village church, but the structure itself is impressive, albeit one which has clearly been renovated many times. Fragments of ancient frescoes sit on top of other fragments of even older frescoes. Built in 1120 on top of an existing crypt, the worn tufa is home to six different bells, the history of which is posted outside the entrance. The beautiful crypt is not open to the public, but its shadows can be peered into through iron gates.

Museo Africano
vicolo Pozzo 1, **T** 045 596238. *Tue-Fri 0900-1200, 1500-1800. €4.*
Map 1, B7, p250

Closed for restoration at the time of writing but due to reopen in autumn 2003, the African Museum contains a variety of exhibits taken from the Colombian missions. Founded in 1938, clothes, instruments and tools are an insight into African customs, but also into the colonial attitudes of their collectors.

Castel San Felice and the city walls
Map 1, A8, p250

Near the top of via Fontana del Ferro a worn path along a grassy track branches off to the right. About 150 m up this path there is a t-junction, with paths heading off left and right along the northern section of city wall. This is an area of olive groves which reaches right down into Veronetta. Head left along the walls to reach the remains of Castel San Felice or right to follow the walls south towards the Giardino Giusti. High walls on both sides mean that glimpses of the city below, though spectacular, are fleeting. In both directions the paths rejoin roads back down into the city after 15 minutes or so. For a longer walk, an archway in the wall just after the castle leads to via Castel San Felice and allows you to join up with the walk detailed in Colline Veronese (see p79).

★ Giardino Giusti
2 via Giardino Giusti, **T** 045 8034029, *Apr-Sep 0900-2000, Oct-Mar 0900-1900.* €4.50. *Map 1, C7, p250*

Agostino Giusti, a Venetian knight, planned the Renaissance gardens of Palazzo Giusti in 1570, and they remain true to his original designs today. Behind ornate box hedges, classical statues, fountains and cypress trees (one of which Goethe wrote about) the gardens rise up the hill on terraces and paths to give great views of the city.

Steps from the main avenue lead to a grotto which was once encrusted with glass and shells but now has no more than some grotty, not to mention phallic, stalactites. Above this is a balcony with a twisted face, which was designed to emit flames from its mouth. Spiral stairs lead up to this, and to the higher levels of the garden. Daisies grow on the lawns and paths between trees are, in places, almost wild. This combination of formal and informal gives the Giardino Giusti a friendly, fairytale feel. There are claims that the maze here is one of the oldest in Europe, but until the hedges grow high enough to avoid being stepped over, it will remain unchallenging.

Museo Civico di Storia Naturale

Lungadige Porta Vittoria 9, **T** 045 8079400, **F** 045 8000804, www.museostorianaturaleverona.it *Mon-Thu, Sat 0900-1900, Sun 1400-1900. € 2.10. Map 2, J8, p253*

Covering zoology, botany and prehistory, and all housed in the handsome Renaissance Palazzo Lavezola Pompei, built by Michele Sanmicheli around 1550, Verona's natural history museum is, in the main, a fairly old-fashioned collection of stuffed animals, minerals and fossils in glass cases. There are some interesting exhibits, however, and some of the fossils, in particular, are spectacular. The best and biggest fossils come from Bolca, to the northeast of the city, now 900 m above sea level, but 50 million years ago a steamy combination of sea, islands, volcanoes, and some large scary-looking spiny fish. The geology section has lots of colourful stones in more glass cases, as well as a scale model of Mount Etna. More interestingly, the main staircase has a display of an enormous number of slabs of different varieties and colours of Veronese marble. In the animals section there are the bones of a grizzly bear, a species which lived in caves all along the southern edge of the Alps until the last great glacial expansion 12,000 years ago. On the first floor there are a crocodile skull, two stuffed tigers and some very large spiders as well as the 3.72 m long skull of a fin whale killed after a collision with a ship in the Gulf of Genoa. *Aqua, Terra, Aria* (Water, Earth, Air) is an attempt at a more modern slant on the story of evolution, but really it's more of the same with added sound effects and smart lighting. Back on the ground floor on the way out there is an excellent three-dimensional map of Verona, Lake Garda and the surrounding area.

Chiesa Santo Stefano

piazza Santo Stefano. *Mon, Wed-Sun, 0900-1200, 1600-1800, Tue 0900-1200. Free. Map 2, B6, p252*

The city's cathedral in the latter part of the first millennium, Santo Stefano may have first been built as early as the 5th century. It has an unusual octagonal tower as well as more typical Veronese Romanesque pink and cream alternating tufa and brick. Inside there are works by Domenico Brusasorci – both above the entrance and in the dome. More striking, however, is the ornate white and gold Cappella degli Innocenti, with three spectacular frescoes from 1621, two of which are grotesquely brutal, by Bassetti, Ottini and Orbetto. On opposite walls, two 14th-century sepia frescoes by Giovanni Battista dal Moro show an early understanding of the use of three-dimensional space. The 10th-century crypt, usually kept closed, has remains of 12th- and 13th-century frescoes.

Chiesa San Giorgio in Braida

Lungadige San Giorgio in Braida. *Mon-Sat 0800-1100, 1700-1900. Free. Map 2, B5, p252*

Founded originally as a Benedictine monastery in 1046, San Giorgio was taken over by the Augustinians, and by the time of the Scaligeri domination was an important power base in the city – Scaligeri offspring were occasionally nominated as abbots. The building gained its current shape in the Renaissance with the addition of an imposing dome by Michele Sanmicheli around 1530. The single nave, barrel-vaulted interior has decorated 16th-century side chapels. Works of art of particular note are Paolo Veronese's complicated and colourful masterpiece *The martyrdom of St George*, Tintoretto's *Baptism of Christ* above the entrance and Girolamo dai Libri's *Sacra Conversazione* in the fourth chapel on the left. A red button to the right of the altar illuminates Veronese's painting, but you can't get very close to it. The church's name, *in Braida*, probably refers to the part of the Adige which widens at this point, making it a suitable area for boatsmen and merchants to stop.

● *Steps down to the river from outside San Giorgio lead to a 200 m riverside promenade which curves around to Ponte Pietra and gives some of the best views of the city.*

Colline Veronesi
Map 1, A8, p250

A map ('Carta dei Sentieri sulle Colline Veronesi') produced by *Gruppi Alpinisti Veronesi* of the hills above Verona is available from bookshops in the city for € 3.10. It marks various paths to the north of the city as well as detailing (in English as well as Italian) the **Dorsale delle Frazioni**, a 15-km walk along the hills from Parona to the city's west to Montorio to the east, passing through Quinzano, Avesa, Poiano and Novaglie. Alternatively, a good four-or five-hour circuit follows path '10' from Verona (it can be joined just north of Castel San Felice at the northernmost point of the city walls) to Poiano, either 'D' (the Dorsale delle Frazioni) or the longer, hillier '3' across the hills to Avesa, and route '6' back down into the centre of the city. Most of these paths are traffic-free and are marked (with a blue and yellow square and the number of the route). However, these markings can often disappear at vital moments, and the map mentioned above is highly recommended.

◉ Museums and galleries

- **Centro Internazionale di Fotografia** Often striking photography exhibitions held under the centre of the city in the Scavi Scaligeri, the excavations of ancient Verona, p40.
- **Galleria d'Arte moderna** An interesting permanent collection of modern art in a modern conversion of ancient Palazzo Forti, plus a space for high-profile international exhibitions, p47
- **Museo degli Affreschi** A large collection of frescoes that once adorned the houses and churches of the city, p68.
- **Museo Africano** Spoils of Colombian missions to Africa, p75.
- **Museo Archeologico** Roman statues, carvings, mosaics and remains on the terraces above the Teatro Romano, p71.
- **Museo Canonicale** The church's small collection of art and artefacts, mainly from deconsecrated buildings, p51.
- **Museo di Castelvecchio** The city's main museum has Longobard jewellery, ancient sarcophagi, Renaissance Italian and Flemish paintings and the original equestrian statue of Cangrande I, p57.
- **Museo Civico di Storia Naturale** Stuffed animals and enormous fossils, p77.
- **Museo Lapidario Maffeiano**, An enormous number of inscribed Roman stones, p56.
- **Museo Miniscalchi-Erizzo** A mixed collection of furniture and artefacts in a grand Veronese townhouse, p51.
- **Museo della Radio d'Epoca** Unexpectedly attractive antique radios from all over the world, p70.

Lago di Garda 83

Italy's largest and most popular lake. Olive groves, watersports, walks and package tours.

Valpolicella and Lessinia 91

Wine, walking, waterfalls and a stone bridge.

Soave and the southern plains 96

More wine, villas, hot springs and lots of flat farmland.

Vicenza 99

Showpiece of Renaissance architecture with Palladio's palaces, Duomo and theatre.

Mantova 104

Medieval cobbled squares, Renaissance frescoed palaces, an ancient round church and three interconnecting lakes.

Brescia 109

Fascist architecture, Roman remains, two cathedrals, a castle and some pawn shops.

Lago di Garda

Wide and surrounded by plains at its southern end, progressively narrower and enclosed by mountains to the north, Lake Garda is an exceptionally beautiful place which mass tourism has done its best to blight. It's just about big enough to be able to cope with the hordes of package holidaymakers, especially if you head away from the coastline itself and up into the hills and mountains around its northern end. It's the lake itself most come for, however, and the beaches and lakeside towns and villages have plenty of facilities for watersports and boat trips across the water. If you really want to worship at the altar of 21st-century tourism, or you're with kids who've had their fill of Renaissance Italy, **Gardaland** *offers Italy's most famous escape into a theme park world, complete with rides, queues and assorted rip-offs, see Kids, p212.*

At the southern end of the lake two large towns, **Peschiera** *and* **Desenzano**, *are served by the main Verona-Milan train line as well as frequent buses from Verona. They also offer the best onward travel options to the rest of the lake. There's little to see in either, though Desenzano is the less objectionable. Nearby* **Sirmione** *is similarly over-touristed, though it does have a sight or two to justify its popularity. On a narrow peninsula jutting out into the southern part of the lake, it has sulphurous springs, a Scaligeri castle, and remains which may once have been a Roman spa, or, alternatively, Catullus's villa. Working up the eastern side of the lake,* **Garda, Malcesine** *and* **Torri del Benaco** *are more traditional towns in attractive settings and* **Torbole** *has a thriving windsurfing industry and some surf culture to go with it. Malcesine also has a cable car which takes passengers up to the high slopes of* **Monte Baldo**. *At the top of the lake,* **Riva del Garda** *is a relatively old-fashioned resort, and down the western side* **Limone** *and* **Gardone**, *though touristy, back onto more spectacular and relatively unfrequented hills.*

▸▸ *See Sleeping p127, Eating and drinking p152, Bars and clubs 170*

Sights

Torri del Benaco
Around Verona Map, inside back cover

Possibly the lake's most attractive town, and only an hour by bus from Verona, 'Torri' has a cobbled, pedestrianized old centre, a Scaligeri castle, hills that slope down behind the town, good beaches for swimming, some decent restaurants and great views across to the mountains on the other side.

The walls around the town were enlarged and strengthened during the 14th-century Scaligeri rule of Antonio della Scala, who also built the castle on the ruins of an existing 10th-century castle which stood on the same spot (the west tower is a remnant of this earlier structure). At around the same time the Fisherman's Guild of Torri and Garda (still in existence today) was also founded here and the town became the most important on the lake. The **Castello Scaligeri** (viale Fratelli Lavanda 2, *Jun-Sep, Mon-Sun, 0930-1300, 1630-1930, Apr-May and Oct, 0930-1230, 1430-1800.* € 3, **T/F** 045 6296111) has displays about the Fisherman's Guild as well as olive presses, parts of some of which date back to Roman times, and maps and models of Torri as it once was. The three towers give good views over Torri, and down into the turquoise waters of the lake.

Piazza Calderini surrounds the small, pretty harbour and has some touristy shops and cafés opposite the castle. These continue along the pedestrianized main street, **corso D'Alighieri**, leading to **piazza Umberto I**, an elongated space which leads down to the lake, with some good cafés and pizzerias. Via C Battisti leads to piazza della Chiesa, and the town's church. Towards the northern end of the town a good, but narrow, shingle beach fills up quickly on summer weekends. To the south the **Lido** is a pay beach with a hip-hop and R'n'B based disco on Friday and Saturday evenings in summer from 2230 (viale Marconi 4, **T** 045 6290405).

● Baia delle Sirene on the Punta San Vigilio (see below), one of the Lake's best swimming spots, is only about a five-minute bus journey south of Torri (€ 1.60 single).

Baia delle Sirene
Pay beach € 9 a day. Around Verona Map, inside back cover

On the Punta San Vigilio, between Garda and Torri del Benaco, an attractive small bay has both paying and free beaches and is an excellent place for swimming. The pay beach has grassy terraces with trees curving around a shingle beach. The free beach can be reached by walking north along the coast road for about 250 m to where a steep path (signposted "free entrance to mermaid bay" in English) leads down to a stonier, less tidy beach. There are olive trees to give shade though, and rocks from which it is safe to dive. A floating snack bar visits both beaches in season, selling ice-creams, drinks and sandwiches.

Malcesine
Around Verona Map, inside back cover

With some favourable winds for sailing and windsurfing, and a slickly modern cable car which whisks passengers up to the top of Monte Baldo (see below), Malcesine attracts a slightly more active kind of tourist, but also an enormous number of package tourists who cram its narrow sloping streets and never get more than a few hundred metres from the top of the cable car. The town itself, jutting out into the lake on a point, and with a castle used by both the Scaligeri and Visconti families, is a pretty, medieval place when you manage to scratch below the flip-flop shops.

The **Castello Scaligeri** (**T/F** 045 6570333, www.malcesinepiu.it *Apr-Nov, Mon-Sun 0930-2000, last entrance 1930, Dec-Mar, Sat, Sun and holidays 0930-2000, last entrance*

Whatever floats your boat
A summer day on one of Lake Garda's beaches is punctuated by the occasional visits of the ice-cream boat.

1930. € 4) in a prominent position overlooking the lake, has, like that of Torri, a tower which predates the della Scala fortifications. The castle was under the control of the Veronese rulers betweem 1277 and 1387. Since that time it has also been owned by the Visconti family and by the Venetians. In 1786 Goethe was arrested on suspicion of being a spy after making sketches of the castle. There is a sprawling old-fashioned museum which focuses primarily on geology and natural history with dead bugs and an assortment of stuffed animals and birds. There is also a temporary exhibition space used for photographic exhibitions and the like.

▶ Garda winds

The special topography of Lake Garda brings about some special geographic effects, not least the winds which Torbole has used to such good advantage to create a thriving windsurfing industry and to hold world championships.

The *Pelèr* or *Suer* wind blows from the north across the northern half of the lake and is one of Garda's most benign winds. Blowing from the early hours of the morning, it results from the night-time cooling of the rocky mountains and the sinking of air down the Garda valley. The wind is usually gone by mid-morning or midday. It produces some waves but is said to bring good weather. The *Ora* wind blows from the south, from around lunchtime until sunset, and is caused by the sun heating up the mountain ranges to the north, making the air there rise, and sucking in air from the Po plain through the narrowing Garda valley. The *Balì* or *Balinot* wind is less common, but sometimes happens after snowfall in winter. Blowing down the Ballino valley near Riva, it can cause big waves.

The town is mostly cobbled and pedestrianized, with narrow sloping streets which lead down to the sea. **Piazza Giglielmo Marconi** is busy and touristy, **piazza Donquirico Turazza** is smaller, with trees and a couple of decent cafés. **Piazza Magenta Gia Porto Vecchio** is the most picturesque of all, and has modern sculptures which sit against a backdrop of lapping water.

▶ Dedicated followers of fascism

On the southwestern edge of Lake Garda, Salò is a small town with a 15th-century cathedral, built when it was an important strategic location. Otherwise it is a fairly unremarkable place. For two years at the end of the Second World War, however, it became the capital of Italy, and gave its name to the ill-fated Salò Republic.

On the 12 June 1943, Mussolini, the Italian leader, was given a vote of no confidence and was removed from office and arrested on the orders of the king. However, after the Germans invaded in the September of that year, Mussolini was freed and taken to Hitler. He returned 10 days later to build a new power base on the shores of Lake Garda.

The Duce, his wife, their sons and grandchildren all lived in the Villa Feltrinelli, and Mussolini's mistress (also rescued from imprisonment by the Germans) stayed nearby, reputedly on direct orders from Hitler. Government ministries were set up in various villas between Salò and Gargano. The Salò Republic was an abject failure, and its name is now synonymous with ineffective fascist thuggery in Italy. Mussolini was by this point little more than a puppet of Hitler's, and a rather flimsy first line of defence of Germany's southern borders. As the allies advanced, Mussolini was shot trying to escape into Switzerland in April 1945.

Thirty years later, Pier Pasolini used the Salò Republic as the backdrop to his notoriously bleak film, *Salò*. The film, a claustrophobically inhuman look at sadism and fascism, power and corruption, became a controversial cause célèbre. Despite being a film about perversion rather than a perverted film, it remained banned in many places until the 1990s and was controversially re-banned in Australia in 1998. Pasolini himself was murdered weeks after finishing the film.

Monte Baldo

Cable cars leave every 30 mins from piazza Marconi 1, Malcesine,
early Apr-mid-Sep 0800-1900, mid-Sep-mid-Oct 0800-1800,
mid-Oct-early Nov 0800-1700. €14 return, €9 single, cash only.
Station **T** 045 7400206. *Around Verona Map, inside back cover*

Ridging along much of the eastern side of Lake Garda, Monte
Baldo separates the lake from the Val d'Adige, the valley of the
river which flows through Verona. The modern **Funivia
Malcesine** (Malcesine cable car) is the simplest and most
spectacular way to get to the summit of Monte Baldo, though if
you have your own transport, there are various places along the
lake from which its slopes are accessible. The cable car climbs
from 100 m to 1750 m in around 15 minutes with a break in the
middle. On the upper section the cars revolve slowly to give a
spectacular panorama of the lake and its surrounding mountains.

The highest part of the mountain is at Cima Valdritta to the
south, at 2218 m and there are a few ski lifts dotted around,
including one above Brenzone, though a network from the top of
the Malcesine cable car route at Tratto Spino covers 11 km of
runs. In summer, it's walking territory, and plenty of paths wind
their way around the peaks, with vertiginous views down to both
east and west. In spring and summer there is a profusion of wild
flowers, and eagles, chamois and marmots are among the
wildlife you might see. Maps of paths are available from the
Malcesine tourist information office, though sometimes the
paths they mark are less than clear. It's also possible to rent bikes

! In the early 15th century, when the Milanese Visconti family
controlled Lake Garda, the Venetians sailed a fleet of 31 boats
from the Adriatic, up the Adige, carried them through the
valley of Santa Lucia at the northern end of the lake, and
launched them on the lake, defeating the Milanese troops.

at the bottom cable car station, carry them to the top and cycle down. The walk down takes around two and a half hours from the top, around an hour from the halfway station.

Torbole
Around Verona Map, inside back cover See also Sports, p203

At the northern end of the lake, separated from its larger and more famous neighbour Riva del Garda by the Sarca river and the high plateau of Monte Brione, Torbole is famous for its windsurfing, and international championships are held here. Windsurfing is, however, just one aspect of a wide range of sportiness which happens at Torbole – everything from beach volleyball to sailing, and the atmosphere is younger and hipper than at Riva. Which is not to say that there isn't also a fair proportion of middle-aged spread, and outside of high season and big competitions the place is less vibrant than you might expect. The old town is small but reasonably attractive, its position at the top of the lake is spectacular, and as a place to learn to windsurf or sail it takes some beating. There are also some good beaches and excellent views down the lake.

The **Chiesa di Sant'Andrea**, rebuilt in the 18th century after being destroyed by French troops in 1703, is back from the lake up winding alleys and is worth a visit for the views. More spectacular, but much more of a climb, the **Castello Penede** is an ancient ruin perched high and precariously above the town in a spot which was once used by the Romans. Another interesting excursion is to the **Marmitte dei Giganti** (Giants' kettles), en route to Nago. These enormous glacial basins were carved out of the rocks between 130,000 and 12,000 years ago.

Valpolicella and Lessinia

Immediately to the north of Verona the hills start to rise upwards towards the Parco Naturale Regionale della Lessinia, a 10,000 ha national park of hills, valleys, cherrry trees and marble quarries topped by a small ski resort. To the west the Adige river cuts between this area of hills and Monte Baldo, bending north as you head upstream towards the Alps. Nestled inside this bend of the river, the valleys of the Valpolicella area, protected from bad weather, are ideal for growing grapes.

▸▸ *See Sleeping p129, Eating and drinking p156*

Sights

Valpolicella

Around Verona Map, inside back cover

A rich, and in places surprisingly built-up, area of valleys at the foot of the Lessinia hills, Valpolicella is mostly taken up with the business of wine-making, though among the vineyards are also olive groves and plenty of cherry trees which blanket the area in white blossom in spring. Wine may have been made here as early as the 8th century BC. Although the Valpolicella wine region extends east towards the Soave region, Valpolicella Classico comes only from the three valleys of Negrar, Marano and Fumane, with streams which all feed into the Adige. The temperate micro-climate is affected by the protection of the high Lessinia hills to the north and Lake Garda to the west.

Among its towns, San Pietro in Cariano, Fumane, and Negrar have the most to offer, though this is seldom much more than an attractive piazza, a church and a few wine bars and restaurants. There are more than fifty winemakers in Valpolicella, some of which have beautiful old villas in the midst of their vineyards. The best way to see the area is to visit the actual vineyards themselves – most are open to the public at least some of the time, or by appointment, for tours and tastings. For example, the Serègo Alighieri estate in Gargagnago, still owned by descendants of Dante, **T** 045 7703622, **F** 045 7703523, www.seregoalighieri.it, *open daily, 1000-1800*. Olive oil and jams are also produced. The tourist information office in San Pietro in Cariano has lists of hours and contacts. If you're here in April, the *Magnalonga* walking eating and drinking event (see p184) makes an excellent introduction to the area.

In Negrar, the formal gardens of Villa Rizzardi, the **Giardino di Pojega**, are open to the public in summer, with wine tasting in groups by appointment (**T** 045 7210028, **F** 045 7210704, www.guerrieri-rizzardi.com *Apr-Oct, Tue and Wed 1500-1900, Thu-Sun 1100-1900*).

San Pietro in Cariano has two villas open to the public, Buri-Avanzi (**T** 045 7701102) and Saibante-Monga (**T** 045 7701042).

Parco delle Cascate di Molina
Around Verona Map, inside back cover

Heading up the valley from Fumane the wooded hillsides sloping down to the stream of *il progno* get progressively closer together, and the water cascades down a series of waterfalls through the Parco delle Cascate di Molina. The east-west **Val Sorda**, which joins the main valley below the waterfalls, is even narrower, becoming a gorge for several miles where the water has cut sharply down into the soft limestone. A path up the Val Sorda is spectacular but only recommended for the agile. Good shoes are essential, though metal rope and handles set into the rock do give extra support along the most difficult parts. Once the path exits the gorge onto the Lessinia plateau above, you can walk around through Cerna and Spiazzo to Molina and back down the main valley, Vajo di Fumane.

⬤ *Bar Trattoria Valsorda (see p156) has a car park and is a convenient starting point for walks up the surrounding valleys and gorges for those with their own transport.*

Molina

Bus 5-6 from Verona. Check www.apt.vr.it for timetables.
Around Verona Map, inside back cover

North of Fumane on the western edge of Lessinia, Molina is surrounded by hills and the steeply cut valleys and waterfalls of the **Parco delle Cascate di Molina** (see above).

Molina is also home to the **Museo Botanico della Lessinia** (**T** 045 7720222, *Jul-Aug, Tue-Sun 1000-1200, 1500-1800, otherwise by appointment*), with information and displays about the irises, orchids and other plants of the area.

Ponte di Veja

7 km southeast of Sant'Anna d'Alfaedo. *Around Verona Map*

Lessinia's most famous sight is Europe's biggest natural bridge – an enormous arch of stone high above the valley below. Thirty metres high and 47 m long, paths enable visitors to walk both under and over what once would have been the entrance to a giant cavern. Other caves around the base of the bridge contain evidence of prehistoric human habitation, as well as that of bears. The path which passes these caves then winds up through woods back around to the top of the bridge.

...if you want to order a cappuccino with brioche you should try to arrive before ten thirty. Of course, you could still order the same things later, but this would be a declaration of your foreignness

Tim Parks, *Italian Neighbours*, 1992

Bosco Chiesanuova

via Spiazzi 4. *Bus 10 from Verona's bus station goes to Bosco Chiesanuova every hour or two. Timetable available at www.apt.vr.it Around Verona Map, inside back cover*

The nearest that Lessinia gets to having a centre, and home to its only tourist information office (see p28), Bosco Chiesanuova is reachable by bus from Verona, and is a good centre for exploring the surrounding hills. There is also a large, year-round, outdoor ice-skating rink.

The town centres around the pedestrianized piazza della Chiesa, with cafés, shops and the imposing church itself, built in 1850. The tourist information office has plenty of information about surrounding walks and mountain bike trails. The small **Museo Etnografico** (**T** 045 6780280. *Jul-Aug, Tue, Fri, Sat and Sun, 1630-1830, Sep-Jun, Sat and Sun only, 1630-1830*) deals with the history of human interaction with Lessinia, from the history of skiing to the weaving of wool.

The **Palaghiaccio** (ice rink) is further down the hill (**T** 045 7050698, *closed Mon in winter. Seasonal timetable, ring or check www.boscochiesanuova.net for times. €8 entrance and skate hire*).

San Giorgio

Skiing information **T** 045 6784001. *Downhill, prices start at €8 for a 2-hour pass. Cross-country from €4 per day.*

With three lifts, a floodlit piste, 5 km of guaranteed snow and nearly 25 km of piste for *sci fondo* (cross-country skiing), San Giorgio, not Italy's most picturesque ski resort, is nevertheless reasonably well-equipped for a day or two on the slopes. There are also some marked paths through the snow for those on foot. Skis of both downhill and cross-country varieties are available to hire. Should you want to stay, the ugly Hotel Sporting (**T** 340 9771079, info.hotelsporting@libero.net) has rooms.

Soave and the southern plains

The white wine area of Soave, to the east of Verona, centres around the attractive walled town of Soave itself, complete with the obligatory Scaligeri castle, narrow winding medieval streets and wine bars. To the south of the city, beyond its sprawling industrial area, towns are liberally sprinkled across a landscape of flat crop-growing plains. The most interesting of these is Valeggio, to the west, on the river Mincio, a town which has developed for itself the reputation of a culinary centre.

▸▸ *See Eating and drinking p158*

 ## Sights

Soave

Buses arrive and depart from the same bus stop opposite Porta Verona, just to the south of the centro storico.

The ancient walls of Soave are still intact, and they enclose a quiet medieval town with sloping cobbled streets, a castle and plenty of attractive wine bars, all selling an enormous selection of local white wine. Though the castle is known as the **Castello Scaligeri** (**T** 045 7680036, *Tue-Sun 0900-1200, 1500-1830, €4.50*) the original structure predates its 13th-century Scaligeri restoration by some three centuries. The old centre is small, with most of the attractive buildings along via Roma, which rises up the hill from Porta Verona, one of the original 14th-century gates into the walled town. The attractive **piazza dell'Antenna** at the top of the hill is the centre of the town, with the 14th-century Palazzo di Giustizia, now home to a classy restaurant, to the north, the 15th-century Palazzo Cavalli to the east, and the Palazzo Pullici (15th century) to the west. The castle is just to the northeast of here, past the Chiesa dei

Domenicani up the cobbled via Castello. From here there are good views north over the Soave vineyards to the Lessinia hills beyond.

Antiche Terme di Giunone

via delle Terme 1, Caldiero, **T** 045 6151288, www.termedigiunone.it *Jun-Aug 0900-2000, May and Sep 1100-1800. €8.50, kids under 14 €4. Bus 21 or 30 goes approximately every half an hour from Verona station.*

Between Soave and Verona, the hot springs at Caldiero emerge from the ground at a constant 27°C. Known as the Terme di Giunone, they have been used for centuries to provide warm water for swimming pools and two of the 15th-century pools are still open, though they have now been added to by a modern olympic pool, a kids' pool and another small pool with a waterfall. It's the two ancient pools which are the most attractive though, especially the Brentella pool, which is circular, and surrounded by worn stone steps. The waters have supposedly therapeutic qualities. On summer Fridays and Saturdays the complex becomes a disco: *Village*, with the pool open to 0200, house music, and even (in 2003 at least) James Brown putting in a visit (**T** 349 1954626, www.flipperhouse.it).

Vallegio sul Mincio

Around Verona Map, inside back cover

South of Lake Garda, on the Mincio river which flows out of it, Valeggio was, despite its **Castello Scaligeri**, a fairly anonymous town until its population decided to use their home-cooking skills to start up restaurants and *trattorie*. The town now has the reputation for being the place where you can find the best traditional cooking in the region, and is packed full of family-run restaurants. Locals will tell you that you can't go far wrong if you come here for a meal, and they are probably right – food here is handmade using fresh ingredients by people who care and know about what they're doing. For a couple of pointers, however, see p133.

Borghetto, just down the road, is pretty, but also more touristy. With lots of old waterwheels from mills no longer in operation, and the waters of the Mincio around and under nearly every corner, it is very picturesque. There are more views up to the Castello, with its ancient crumbling walls, and plenty of waterside cafés and restaurants, but it is also crammed with bijou shops selling sickly sweet oil paintings, soap and essential oils.

Parco Giardino Sigurtà

Valeggio sul Mincio, **T** 045 6371033, **F** 045 6370959, www.sigurta.it *Mar-Nov, Mon-Sun 0900-1900. €8, children under 14 €5.50, children under 5 free. Bicycle hire, €3 first hour, €1.50 each subsequent half hour. Golf carts €12 first hour, €6 each subsequent half hour. Mini train €2. Around Verona Map, inside back cover*

Twenty gardeners and an enormous quantity of water keep this park verdant and preened, though it has its wilder parts, too. The sloping lawns and trees and expansive areas of flowers extend to 50 ha of beautiful parkland, and are a great place for a picnic. Originally the Giardino Sigurtà was the garden of Villa Maffei, designed by Pellesina, a student of Palladio, in 1617, and at one time in the mid-19th century it was the headquarters of Napoleon III. It has one of Italy's few grass tennis courts, irises, tulips and cyclamen among its 30,000 plants, a rose-bordered avenue with fantastic views of Valleggio's Castello Scaligeri, a mini ivy-covered castle, turtles, goats, deer and goldfish . There are plenty of drink and ice-cream stands, too, and in the heat of summer, plenty of sprinklers under which hot visitors can cool off. A mini-train does a 7 km circuit around the park and you can hire bikes and golf carts. The fairly expensive entry price has the advantage of meaning it doesn't often get too crowded.

Vicenza

*Some of Italy's finest and most influential Renaissance architecture,
much of it built by Palladio (see box, p101) is in the beautiful,
compact, UNESCO-listed, pedestrianized centre of Vicenza. Only just
over half an hour by train from Verona it makes an excellent day trip.
From the station a 5-minute walk up viale Roma takes you to piazzale
de Gasperi and through the della Scala built Porta Castello to the
beginning of* **corso Palladio**, *the city's main shopping street and an
architectural feast, with many buildings by the eponymous architect
himself. To the south, the city's* **Duomo** *was also designed by the
great man, as were several buildings on and around the spectacular
central square,* **piazza dei Signori**. *Palladio's masterpiece is
considered by many to be the* **Teatro Olimpico**, *the theatre at the
far eastern end of* **corso Palladio**, *a blueprint for most of the world's
subsequent theatres. Nearby, Palladio's* **Palazzo Chiericati** *is used
as the city's art gallery.*

▶▶ *See Sleeping p131, Eating and drinking p160*

 Sights

Corso Palladio
Map 3, E2-A8, p254

As in Verona, the layout of Vicenza follows the original Roman
street pattern and corso Palladio was once the *decumanus
maximus* of the Roman town of Vicetia. Aside from the route,
however, little Roman remains and the emphasis is firmly on the
Renaissance, and on 21st-century shopping. Palazzi especially
worth dragging your eyes away from the smart shoe shops for
include **Palazzo Bonin Longare**, **Palazzo Thiene** (designed by
Palladio) and **Casa Cogollo**.

Duomo

piazza Duomo, **T** 0444 320996. *Mon-Fri 1000-1200, 1530-1730, Sat 1030-1200, Sun 1000-1200. Map 3, F3/4, p254*

To the right off corso Palladio as you walk from the porta Castello end is the Duomo, a large striking brick construction sitting in its own piazza. the building was damaged in the Second World War but has been restored. Palladio's dome, built between 1588 and 1574, was joined onto the medieval body of the church, as was the apse in the previous century. A Christian basilica stood on this site as early as the 5th century. Reconstruction and modification was also carried out in the 8th, 9th, 10th and 11th centuries before its later Gothic and Renaissance makeovers.

● *Opposite the Duomo, in the courtyard of the neoclassical Bishop's Palace, is the Loggia Zeno. Built by Bernardino da Milano in 1494 of local stone, it is one of the most elegant examples of Renaissance architecture in Vicenza.*

Piazza dei Signori and piazza delle Biade

Map 3, E5-D6, p254

Vicenza's centre is also its most spectacular spot. You might be forgiven for thinking that these two piazzas, along the northern flank of the hulking **Basilica**, were in fact one. The theoretical dividing line is marked by two pillars near the eastern end of the space, modelled on those in piazza San Marco in Venice. Piazza dei Signori was probably the site of the Roman forum, and remains the focal point of the city today.

The Basilica, also known as the *Palazzo della Ragione*, dominates the piazzas. A judicial rather than religious building, the original Gothic barrel-vaulted structure was built in the mid 15th century by Domenico da Venezia. Palladio's two-storey reinforcing loggia around the building was added a hundred years later, and not finished until 1614, 34 years after his death. His design for the

Design classic

Born in Padua in 1508, Andrea di Pietro della Gondola was named 'Palladio' by a local aristocrat – a reference to the classical Greek goddess Pallas Athene, but also to an angel in Trissino's poem *Italia liberata dai Goti*, Italy Liberated from the Goths – after he moved to Vicenza at the age of 16 and took on the classical influences of the Renaissance.

Apprenticed as a stone-cutter, family connections to Veronese architect Michele Sanmicheli helped his rise to become Italy's most sought-after architect.

16th-century Vicenza had all the factors for a Renaissance building boom. A rich but small city anxious to compete with its big neighbour Venice, Vicenza had plenty of aristocratic families wishing to commission monuments to their wealth and good taste.

More than just rediscovering the classical architectural tenets of Vitruvius and the styles of ancient Rome, Palladio took Renaissance architecture onto a new level. His agenda was humanist, functionality and usability sitting alongside an innovative take on classical grandeur. As the most famous and successful proponent of Italian Renaissance building, he is arguably the most influential architect in the world.

imposing structure includes Doric columns on the ground floor and Ionic columns on the first floor. The hall itself is now used for exhibitions, and is closed at other times.

Opposite the Basilica, the **Loggia del Capitaniato** is smaller, but equally striking. Also known as the *Loggia Bernarda*, Palladio was given the commission to design it in 1571, to mark victory in the Battle of Lepanto. Originally intended to stretch further along the northern side of the square, the building never reached the extent of its design. Erstwhile base of the Venetian rulers of Vicenza, the building is now home to the city council.

The tall slim clock tower of **Torre di Piazza** was originally built in the 12th century but was added to at various points thereafter, reaching its current height of 82 m in the 15th century.

● *To the south of the Basilica, a third piazza, piazza Erbe, has a tower, Torre del Tormento, which was a prison and place of torture in medieval times. To the west, the small piazzetta Palladio has a statue of the man himself.*

Ponte San Paolo
Map 3, F6, p254

South of Vicenza's central piazzas, the Retrone river is crossed by a number of bridges, notably Ponte San Paolo, the original version of which was Roman and carried the *cardo maximus*. There are good views of Gothic buildings and what was once the city's port area.

Teatro Olimpico
piazza Matteotti 11, **T** 0444 222800. *Jul-Aug, Tue-Sun 0900-1900, Sep-Jun 0900-1700. Joint ticket also covers Museo Civico Palazzo Chiericati and the Museo Naturalistico Archeologico, valid for three days, € 7. For music and drama information and ticketing, contact the tourist information office in piazza Matteotti (see p27). At the far eastern end of corso Palladio, off piazza Matteotti. Map 3, A8, p254*

Embodying just about all the aspects of Renaissance architecture, Palladio's masterpiece, designed just before his death in 1580 and completed posthumously by his son Silla, is seen as the world's first modern theatre. The architect's use of perspective is strikingly innovative, converging lines creating a convincing optical illusion of a stage which recedes far into the distance. There are classical motifs and statues, but it is the sense of space which is the theatre's most enduring legacy, the proscenium arch format copied countless times since. After the banning of theatrical productions by the counter-Reformation in the late

Keeping a watchful eye
*Palladio's influence permeates most of Vicenza and his statue stands
proud in the centre of the city.*

16th century the theatre was not regularly used again until after the Second World War. It now hosts regular summer seasons of music and drama.

Museo Civico Palazzo Chiericati

Joint ticket also covers Teatro Olimpico and the Museo Naturalistico Archeologico, valid for three days, €7. Map 3, B/C8, p254

Another grand masterpiece by the ubiquitous architect, the Palazzo Chiericati, also known as the *Pinoteca*, holds the city's art collection. Innovative in its design, Palladio turned around many of the Venetian traditions of layout, for example by placing the hall parallel to the façade instead of perpendicular to it.

The art collection, arranged chronologically, is mainly made up of 16th-century Veneto Renaissance work. Highlights include Lorenzo Lotto's *Madonna col Bambino*, and a crucifixion by Hans Memling, both on the ground floor, and several works in the great hall upstairs, including Veronese's Madonna and Tintoretto's depiction of St Augustine healing the cripples. The hall itself is a deceptively simple room, much admired for its light and sense of space.

Mantova

Almost entirely surrounded by water, Mantova, 35 km south of Verona, is an attractive and evocative place, at least around the network of piazzas that make up the centre of the city. The city has origins deep in the past, with prehistoric settlements beside its lakes. At the end of the first millennium the Canossa family balanced pressure from Church and Empire to make the town an important base in the middle of the Po plain. The city's golden age came under the three hundred years of rule by the Gonzaga family. One of the richest and most important patrons of the Renaissance, they ruled from the 14th until the 17th centuries.

Coming from the south the first part of the old centre you meet is **piazza Mantegna**, *site of the towering Basilica di Sant'Andrea. This leads into* **piazza Erbe**, *still home to a weekly market, and on across* **piazza Broletto** *to* **piazza Sordello**, *the grandest of Mantova's piazzas. At the northern end of this series of cobbled open spaces is the* **Palazzo Ducale**, *the monumental 14th-century complex of the Gonzaga family, incorporating the sturdy* **Castello di San Giorgio** *and Mantegna's stunning masterpiece of Renaissance painting the* **Camera degli Sposi**, *as well as works by Raphael, Pisanello, Rubens and Giulio Romano. Romano was also responsible for both the building and decoration of the grandiose* **Palazzo Te**, *with its dramatic frescoes, particularly in the Sala dei Giganti. Arriving at the station, the city centre is diagonally left, along via Solferino e San Martino and its continuations.*

▸▸ *See Sleeping p131, Eating and drinking p160*

◉ Sights

Piazza Erbe
Map 4, E6, p255

One-time commercial hub of the city, piazza Erbe still has a fruit and vegetable stall, and a bigger market every Thursday morning. Nowadays it's more given over to restaurants and cafés, nestled into its porticoes and spilling out into the open. There is also a clock tower with a beautiful astrological clock, the **Palazzo della Ragione**, built in 1250, and the **Rotunda di San Lorenzo** (*Mon-Fri 1000-1300, 1500-1800, Sat and Sun 1000-1800. Free*), an atmospheric small round church, the oldest in Mantova, dating from the second half of the 11th century. The excellent tourist information centre (see p28) is also here, on the corner with piazza Mantegna.

Piazza Broletto

Museo Tazio Nuvolari e Learco Guerra, piazza Broletto 9, **T** 0376 327929. *Tue, Wed, Fri-Sun 1000-1300, 1530-1830. €3. Map 4, E6, p255*

Through porticoes and arches, the way north through the centre of Mantova opens out again in piazza Broletto, with more palaces, the **Arengario**, complete with arch, and the **Palazzo del Podestà**. Set into the latter is a seated 13th-century statue of Virgil, the classical poet whom the city claims as its own. This statue is traditionally known as *Vecia Mantua*, the personification of the ancient city. New arrivals to the city are supposed to come and pay their respects to him. Next door the **Museo Tazio Nuvolari e Learco Guerra** is a homage to the two eponymous Mantuan motorcycle champions.

Piazza Sordello

Map 4, D7, p255

The biggest and grandest of Mantua's piazzas, piazza Sordello, to the north of piazza Broletto, contains, in its northern end, the **Duomo**, and, to its east, the enormous Palazzo Ducale complex (see below). As you walk from the arch along the pavement known as the *listone* to the Duomo you also pass, in turn, the 13th-century **Palazzo Bonacolsi**, also known as the Palazzo Castiglioni, and the 18th-century **Palazzo Bianchi**, home of the bishop.

Palazzo Ducale

piazza Sordello, **T/F** 0376 224832. *Tue-Sun, 0845-1915. Ticket office closes 1830. €6.50. Map 4, D7/8, p255*

The Palazzo Ducale is more a conglomeration of buildings than a conventional palace. Built between the 12th and 17th centuries, the complex covers 34,000 sq m and is an awesome illustration of the wealth of the Gonzaga family, whose power base it was. The porticoed buildings facing piazza Sordello are the oldest remaining: the **Magna Domus** and the **Palazzo del Capitano** were built by Guido Bonacolsi, Lord of Mantua, at the beginning of the 14th century. The visitors' entrance to the palace is here, under the arches. The solidly built **Castello di San Giorgio**, facing the lake at the northeast corner of the old city, dates from the end of the 14th century and was built for Francesco I Gonzaga. The palace has around 500 rooms, and, despite the Habsburgs removing 80 works of art in 1630, some excellent paintings, frescoes and tapestries, including works by Raphael and Pisanello. The highlight, however, is Mantegna's extraordinary frescoed Camera Picta, more usually known as the **Camera degli Sposi** (room of the married couple), although its original owner, Lodovico, supposedly slept there alone. Painted between 1465 and 1474, Mantegna's masterpiece depicts family and friends of Lodovico, Emperor Frederik III of the Habsburg Empire, King Christian I of Denmark, buildings, landscapes, animals and even, among the decoration on a pilaster, a self-portrait of Mantegna himself.

Palazzo Te

viale Te, **T** 0376 323266. *Mon 1300-1800, Tue-Sun 0900-1800. Ticket office closes 1730. €8.*

Well signposted from the centre of the city (as "Percorso del Principe", or path of the prince), Palazzo Te is a disappointingly plain half-hour walk to the south. It was built by Giulio Romano as a palace for the Gonzago family. A fine example of a Renaissance villa, Palazzo Te was built between 1525 and 1535. It once stood on an island known as the Te. The artist given the job of frescoing the palace, Romano, apprenticed in Raphael's studio and was considered his finest heir. Federico Gonzago stayed infrequently, however, and the building was used mainly for state occasions, including two visits by Charles V of Spain.

Renaissance town
Mantova's old centre is made up of an interlinked series of cobbled piazzas, with cafés under porticoes.

Impressively grand, the palace is known primarily today for its internal decoration, particularly that of the so-called **Camera dei Giganti**. Romano's frescoes illustrate the myth of the giants being hurled down the mountain by Jupiter for having dared to try to climb Olympus. Dickens complained that the paintings were grotesque, though this seems to be the intention: there are twisted ogres, and the scale and perspective looking up overwhelms and disguises the form of the room. Up in the clouds of Olympus, however, the gods look comparatively normal.

The Camera di Amore e Psiche is another highlight, and the Camera di Cavalli demonstrates the Gonzaga obsession with horses.

Brescia

*Often regarded as an industrial city, an economic powerhouse, and a pallid younger sibling to Milan, Brescia is often passed through, but seldom stopped in, which is a shame – the city has an unexpectedly attractive centre, as well as some excellent restaurants. Its celebrated fascist architecture is an obvious highlight, particularly in **piazza della Vittoria**, but there are also plenty of Renaissance and medieval elements, as well as Roman remains just to the east of the city centre on and nearby the site of the forum in **piazza del Foro**. The focal point of the city is also its most beautiful site: **piazza della Loggia** has the 15th-century **Palazzo della Loggia** dominating one end of it, as well as Venetian loggias and an attractive 24-hour clock. Just to the east of here, **piazza Paolo VI** boasts two cathedrals side by side as well as the **Broletto**, one of the city's oldest buildings, incorporating a clock tower.*

▸▸ *See Sleeping p132, Eating and drinking p162*

 Sights

Piazza della Loggia
Map 5, C1/2, p256

The heart of the city is the piazza della Loggia, in turn dominated by the **Palazzo della Loggia** itself. Now used as the town hall, the palace, with an upper part designed by Sansovino with consultations from Palladio, was completed in 1570, 78 years after the laying of the foundation stone. The massive and distinctive rectangular cupola, made of sheets of lead, was added in 1908, following the original 16th-century design. The original roof was destroyed in a fire in 1575 which also destroyed many works of art, including some by Titian. The Salone Vanvitelli, at the top of the palace's grand 1902 staircase, is used for temporary exhibitions and is open to the public. On the south side of the square, between two 15th-century buildings that once housed pawnbrokers, is an attractive Venetian-style loggia. In the building now used as the tourist information office (see p28) the town council decided in 1480 to set into the walls pieces of Roman inscriptions in stone. They are still there today. The eastern side of the piazza has a beautifully ornate clock tower with a 24-hour clock made in the mid 16th century. Via Cesare Beccaria leads under the central arch under the clock to piazza Paolo VI.

Piazza Paolo VI
Map 5, D3, p256

Piazza Paolo VI has too many parked cars to be considered beautiful, but it has three notable buildings: the **Rotonda** (also known as the *Duomo Vecchio*, the old cathedral), the **Duomo Nuovo**, and the **Broletto**. The Rotonda (*Tue-Fri 0900-1200, 1500-1900, Sat-Sun 0900-1200, 1500-1800*), built at the end of the 11th century, has a surprisingly large, circular interior with an ambulatory and a large, frescoed cupola. The Duomo Nuovo (**T** 030 42714, *Mon-Sat 0730-1200, 1600-1930, Sun 0800-1300, 1600-1930*), is much more austere by comparison. Construction of it started in 1604 but it was not completed until 1825. The 80-m high cupola is the third highest in Italy, but other than the scale of the place there is little to see. The Broletto is a composite of various buildings, including a 12th- or 13th-century tower. Centre of political life when Brescia was a city state, it still houses offices of the council, as well as the police station.

Castello
via del Castello. *Daily 0800-2000. Free. Map 5, A4/5, p256*

Populated since prehistoric times, the hill of Colle Cidneo, now dominated by Brescia's castle, rises steeply above the old centre of the city. There are good views north towards the Alps and south down over the Po plain, though much of the old city is obscured by trees. The castle itself has been reinforced on many occasions since its inception in the 13th century. The Mirabella Tower and the Visconti keep are from the 14th century, whereas the entrance, complete with a drawbridge, is from the 16th century. Inside there is a rather plain garden and two small museums of artefacts and arms. There are two routes up to the top of the castle, a winding circuitous route from piazza del Foro to the east, or a more direct, steeper route from piazza Paolo VI.

Teatro Romano/Tempio Capitolino
piazza del Foro. *Map 5, C5, p256*

Brescia's Roman remains are dishevelled and poorly looked after. The Capitolium temple, discovered in 1823, was partially rebuilt and sits in a closed area at the north of piazza del Foro. The Teatro Romano just to the east is, after Verona's, the second largest Roman theatre in Northern Italy. Half buried under a mix of earth, weeds, corrugated iron, rusting scaffolding and cement mixers, it would once have held around 15,000 spectators.

Santa Giulia – Museo della Città
via dei Musei 81B, **T** 030 2977834, www.asm.brescia.it/musei
Jun-Sep 1000-1800, Oct-May 0930-1730. €8. Map 5, C6, p256

The ex-monastery of Santa Giulia, founded in 753 AD by Longobard king Desiderio, holds Brescia's city museum and also has a large grassy Renaissance cloister. Museum highlights are a jewel-encrusted cross beloning to Desiderio himself, a finely carved 4th-century *lipsanoteca* (a box for holding relics) and various Roman artefacts and statues, many found in the excavations of the city's Roman temple and theatre.

Piazza della Vittoria
Map 5, D2, p256

The stark, modern grandiosity of the fascist-era architecture of piazza della Vittoria contrasts completely with neighbouring piazza della Loggia. Designed by Marcello Piacentini, the piazza was inaugurated in 1932, after the old buildings which had stood here previously had been knocked down. The post office dominates, and shiny white marble loggias echo their more antique counterparts.

Sleeping

Verona's disproportionate numbers of day-trippers from Lake Garda means that it is relatively poorly equipped with hotels, most of which fill up, and raise their prices, with lightning speed during opera season. Most hotels drop their prices by a third or more outside of high season and it's often possible to find rooms at reasonable rates right in the centre. Most hotels are in the old centre, and around piazza Bra. Veronetta, which would make a good base, has no hotels at all, though the beautiful, if slightly rigorous, hostel is here, up on the hill of San Pietro. The campsite, further up the same hill, is another option, and a marginally cooler one in the heat of summer. Most hotels, certainly from mid-range upwards, have air-conditioning. Bed and breakfast is a growing sector, though standards vary. Tourist information can provide a brochure listing private rooms. The free room-finding and booking service near piazza Bra (see p115) is geared to the upper end of the hotel market.

€ **Sleeping codes**

Price

AL	€350 and over	**D**	€100-149
A	€250-349	**E**	€75-99
B	€200-249	**F**	€50-74
C	€150-199	**G**	€49 and under

Prices are for a double room in high season. Breakfast is included unless otherwise stated.

The local agriturismo organization produces a brochure of the possibilities for staying in the countryside around the city. It also includes some useful information about local areas. www.agriturismoverona.it

High in the hills and mountains, a network of *rifugi* provide very basic but cheap accommodation. Often without electricity or anything in the way of luxuries, they are little more than bunk barns but are usually in spectacular positions. Check local tourist information offices or www.rifugi.it for details.

Room-finding service

Cooperativa Albergatori Veronesi, via Patuzzi 5, **T** 045 8009844, www.cav.vr.it *Mon-Sat 0900-1930, Sun 1400-1900. Between via Leoncino and via Anfiteatro, behind the Arena. Map 2, J5, p252* This helpful office can find and book rooms at any of their affiliated hotels (which means most of those with three stars or more, and some two-star establishments, too). They have a free brochure and do not charge commission.

Centro storico

Hotels

AL Albergo Due Torri, piazza Sant'Anastasia 4, **T** 045 595044,
F 045 8004130, www.baglionihotels.com *Map 2, E6, p252* Taking
up one side of piazza Sant'Anastasia, the large, plush Due Torri,
Verona's most expensive hotel, looks across to the church of San
Pietro Martire. The big reception area, with jousting murals, marble
columns and heavy drapes, is slightly Carry On Up The Via
Postumia in style. The building is 13th century, though much of the
ancient feel of the place from the days when Mozart, Goethe and
Garibaldi stayed here has been lost, replaced by a rather generic
form of luxuriousness. The 90 rooms are all big, however and
there's no scrimping on furnishings or facilities.

AL Gabbia D'Oro, corso Porta Borsari 4a, **T** 045 8003060, F 045
590293, gabbiadoro@easynet.it Breakfast extra € 23 during opera
season. *Map 2, F5, p252* In possibly the best position in town, at
the end of corso Porta Borsari, a stone's throw away from piazza
Erbe and opposite one of Verona's best cake shops, the Gabbia
D'Oro has an understated façade, and an interior that smells of
exclusivity from the minute you walk through the door. Richly
decorated without being overdone, it retains some medieval
features such as areas of bare walls and wooden beams alongside
the pewter, mahogany and fine carpets. Rooms are similarly plush,
and bathrooms are all marble and chrome. None of this, however,
makes the supercilious staff any more approachable.

B Accademia, via Scala 12, **T** 045 596222, **F** 045 8008440.
Map 2, H5, p252 With an interior design set somewhere around the
1970s, the Accademia has lots of gold, mirrors, chandeliers, marble,
dark wood and the occasional incongruous ancient column. Rooms,

some of which are generously large, face either a green internal terrace or out onto the street, some straight onto via Mazzini itself, bu the windows are very effective at blocking out the noise. Out of high season there is a business-orientated feel to the place.

C **Touring**, via Q Sella 5, **T** 045 590944, **F** 045 590290. *Map 2, G5, p252* Five floors, two non-smoking, make up this large but friendly hotel near the centre of the city. Rooms have firm beds, flowery wallpaper and fairly plain generic hotel decor. There are no great views and only a handful of balconies, but the facilities are good. All rooms have radios and air-conditioning, and there is a buffet breakfast.

C **Victoria**, via Adua 8, **T** 045 590566, **F** 045 590155, hotel.victoria@ifinet.it *Map 2, G4, p252* Not far from corso Porta Borsari, the hotel Victoria has a fairly modern businesslike feel, despite its claims to possessing 'the charm of ancient noble palaces'. Rooms are smart but not especially memorable. It's well equipped though, with all rooms having computers and posh marble bathrooms and some having big stone balconies and jacuzzis.

D **Antica Porta Leona**, corticella Leoni 3, **T** 045 595499, **F** 045 595214. www.anticaportaleona.com *Map 2, H6, p252* Set back from via Leoni up a quiet side street, Antica Porta Leona is a handsome hotel, with geranium-hung balconies and fading grey shutters. Inside, apart from an excessive use of burgundy, rooms are plain but reasonably spacious. Bathrooms are on the small side.

D **Aurora**, piazza Erbe, **T** 045 594717, **F** 045 8010860. *Map 2, F5, p252* In a stunning position overlooking piazza Erbe yet set back from its noise, with a great sunny terrace on which to enjoy the excellent buffet breakfast, and with plain but attractive air-conditioned en-suite rooms, the helpful and friendly Aurora is hard to beat in just about every respect and is excellent value for money. Only three rooms look onto the piazza directly, but others of the nineteen have almost equally good views. Those facing the other direction are quieter.

F Locanda Catullo, via Valerio Catullo 1, **T** 045 8002786, **F** 045 596987, locandacatullo@tiscali.it No breakfast, cash only. *Map 2, H3, p252* Surprisingly central for such a cheap hotel, the second-floor Catullo is up an alleyway just around the corner from via Mazzini. It has few added extras and makes a big deal over the fact that they won't look after your luggage for you. However, rooms and corridors are spacious, if plain. Some cheaper rooms lack en-suite bathrooms. Reception is open from 0900-2300 only and there is no lift.

South of the centro storico

Many of the city's hotels cluster around piazza Bra, though there are also several along the busy corso Porta Nuova (the main road to the station). Generally, the further south you go, the less pleasant the surroundings.

Hotels

B Firenze, corso Porta Nuova 88, **T** 045 8011510, **F** 045 8030374, www.hotelfirenze.it *Map 1, F4, p250* Part of the Best Western group, the hotel Firenze has some surprisingly good prints in its foyer, but it's otherwise very much standard, uninspiring fare. It's comfortable and spacious, well equipped for business and convenient for the station, but also bland. Service is somewhat down in the mouth and, on balance, rooms are overpriced.

B Giberti, via Giberti 7, **T** 045 8006900, **F** 045 8001955, www.hotelgiberti.it *Map 1, F3, p250* An enormous, shiny, modern building, when hotel Giberti claims to be "right in the centre of Verona", it means the Verona of ugly, concrete tower blocks near the station. Inside it's very smart, however, with water tumbling down a sculpture just inside the door and lots of white leather and columns in the open reception area. The 80 rooms are furnished in a mid-20th-century style, with polished wooden floors and marble bathrooms and the whole place has a businesslike feel.

B Grand, corso Porta Nuova, **T** 045 595600, **F** 045 596385 www.grandhotel.vr.it *Map 1, G4, p250* With its striking, fascist-era, Liberty-style façade and ornate balconies, this hotel is indeed grand, with 62 rooms, walnut doors, free internet connections for those with laptops, a large breakfast room with a generous buffet breakfast and English-language newspapers. The courtyard and garden are attractive too, with sculptures, grass, sun-loungers and a waterfall which just about blocks out the sound of the air-conditioning pumps. It's also convenient for the station, though it's a fair walk from most of Verona's main attractions.

B San Luca, via Volto San Luca 8, **T** 045 591333, **F** 045 8002143, www.hotelsanluca.it *Map 2, K2, p252* On a street off the top of corso Porta Nuova, San Luca is, externally at least, one of Verona's uglier hotels. Inside, however, it's surprisingly inoffensive as well as being personable. It's also spotlessly clean and tidy, well equipped, and although it's on the less interesting side of piazza Bra, it's not at all far from the action. For those who like their hotels modern, plain and efficient, and aren't too worried about an air of middle age hanging over the place, it might be the answer.

C Bologna, piazzetta Scalette Rubiani 3, **T** 045 8006830, **F** 045 8010602 www.hotelbologna.vr.it *Map 2, I4, p252* The building housing this hotel just off the corner of piazza Bra apparently dates back to 1200, but there's little sign of it in the anodyne design of this mid-range, middle-of-the-road hotel. It's a great position to be in, however, in a relatively quiet street but close enough for piazza Bra to be seen out of the windows of many rooms. You can rent a car from the hotel for €52 a day. Generous buffet breakfasts also go some way to making up for the ugly carpets, the brown furniture and the pink bedcovers.

C **Colomba d'Oro**, via C Cattaneo 10, **T** 045 595300, **F** 045 594974, www.colombahotel.com *Map 2, I3, p252* With an extravagantly frescoed reception area and a velvet-lined lift, the Colomba makes its intentions clear from the start. Relatively plain rooms, however, don't quite live up to this start, though they do have attractive stained wood furniture, iron-framed beds, and all bathrooms have baths.

C **De' Capuleti**, via del Pontiere 26, **T** 045 8000154, **F** 045 8032970, capuleti@easy1.easynet.it *Map 1, F6, p250* Despite suffering slightly from the inevitable corporate feel that comes from being a part of the Best Western group, De' Capuleti manages to be surprisingly stylish, with exposed stone walls, beams, wooden floors, tasteful art, shiny desks, carefully placed vases, flowers, and fresh fruit in rooms. Opposite Juliet's tomb, it becomes tourist-orientated in summer, but is business-based out of season.

C **Giulietta E Romeo**, vicolo Tre Marchetti 3, **T** 045 8003554, **F** 045 8010862, www.giuliettaeromeo.com *Map 2, I5, p252* Almost in the shadow of the Arena, this is a smart, friendly and efficient hotel with all the facilities you'd expect from a three-star establishment (such as air-conditioning and satellite TV) but without much character. Corridors and stairs have a particularly nasty yellow sponge effect finish, but rooms are a bit better with muted colours and grey-tiled bathrooms.

C **Mastino**, corso Porta Nuova 16, **T** 045 595388, **F** 045 597718, hotelmastino@alinet.it *Map 2, K2, p252* Hotel Mastino is beside and above Verona's main branch of MacDonald's. Strangely, the illustrious fast-food restaurant is missing from photos in the hotel's brochure. Fast food aside, however, it's not a bad place to stay – near to piazza Bra and reasonably attractively kitted out as long as you can put up with the bas-relief cupids on the walls. Rooms are comfortable, modern and largely in pastel shades, some with wooden floors.

C **Milano**, via Tre Marchetti 11, **T** 045 591692, **F** 045 8011299. *Map 2, I4, p252* Unless you nod off during the opera, this is as close as you'll get to sleeping in the Arena itself. However, despite its position it's a plain sort of place, modern and efficient but lacking in character and smiles. The visual style is mainly 1970s – lots of wood laminate and pale leather. Beds are big and there's a garage, but breakfasts, like the place as a whole, can be slightly lacklustre. Prices drop significantly out of high season, when the position, presumably, is less of an advantage.

C **Verona**, corso Porta Nuova 47/49, **T** 045 595944, **F** 045 594391, www.hotelverona.it *Map 2, L2, p252* Hotel Verona is just about the only modern hotel in the city to go for the stylish rather than the bland look, and it is a trick it more or less pulls off. Refurbished in 2001, the reception area has a cool minimalist look with lots of sliding glass, views to greenery behind, and background piano music. Even the brochure has a matt silver finish, with expensive photos and slightly risqué quotes such as Nietzsche's "When virtue has slept, it awakes refreshed." This ambition is not quite carried through to the rooms, which are less striking, though still attractive and comfortable. Rooms facing corso Porta Nuova have balconies, though those at the back, overlooking a courtyard garden behind, are quieter. Rooms also come with a freshly filled fruitbowl.

D Cavour, vicolo Chiodo 4, **T** 045 590166, **F** 045 590508. *Buffet breakfast in high season, € 11 extra, standard breakfast in low season, € 5 extra. Map 2, I2, p252* A friendly, eager-to-please, family-run place, half of the Cavour has been refurbished in an attractive, 'medieval' stye, with exposed wooden beams and ivy-clad balconies overlooking a small, quiet, internal courtyard, where breakfast can be eaten. The rest of the place is more regularly bland in design, but not unpleasant, and it's close to both piazza Bra and Castelvecchio.

D Europa, via Roma 8, **T** 045 594744, **F** 045 8001852, www.veronahoteleuropa.com *Map 2, J3, p252* A modern-looking building in a great position on the corner of via Roma and via Teatro Filarmonico and facing towards piazza Bra, Europa is slightly corporate in feel and rooms are generally ugly-1980s in style.The hotel is also used by some tour operators, but it has all mod cons, offers a buffet breakfast each morning, and is only 50 m from piazza Bra.

D Residence Hotel Castelvecchio, corso Cavour 46/48, **T** 045 594755, **F** 045 595304, gcanossa@libero.it *Map 2, H3, p252* Mostly made up of apartments with four beds and big rooms, the friendly RHC is a particularly good option for families or groups. Apartments have small kitchens, big sitting rooms, very yellow bathrooms, and are airy and spacious. There is a buffet breakfast and some rooms have views over the Adige and Castelvecchio.

D Sanmicheli, via Valverde, **T** 045 8003749, **F** 045 8004508, fosco.dardi@tin.it *Map 2, L2, p252* Another slightly anonymous hotel south of piazza Bra, Sanmicheli at least is in a reasonably attractive building facing some trees. Rooms are all en suite and inoffensive, with white walls , floral bedcovers and predictable reproductions on the walls.

D **Scalzi**, via C Scalzi 5, **T** 045 590422, **F** 045 590069, www.hotelscalzi.it *Map 1, F3, p250* A good value, family-run two-star hotel, Scalzi has some exposed beams but is otherwise generic 20th-century Italian in style. There are an unusual number of single rooms, and some without en-suite facilities. All are air-conditioned however.

D **Siena**, via Marconi 41, **T** 045 8003074, **F** 045 8002182. *Map 1, F4, p250* Complete with dusty plastic flowers, a slightly bumpy lift and staff who look like they, too, need a bit of fresh air, the Siena has a distinctly tired aspect. There's a quiet internal courtyard for breakfast, however, and rooms, all en suite, have good showers and air-conditioning. Decor is indistinctly modern, and in some rooms, overpoweringly yellow.

D **Torcolo**, vicolo Listone 3, **T** 045 8007512, **F** 045 8004058, www.hoteltorcolo.it *Map 2, I3, p252* On a quiet road behind piazza Bra, the all-women run Torcolo has a rare quantity of charm and style in a city with a surfeit of bland hotels. Nineteen rooms on three floors are all individual – those on the third floor, with sloping ceilings, are particularly attractive. Furniture is eclectic, with some beautiful antiques among other more utilitarian pieces. A private collection of modern Italian drawings and paintings lines the corridors, and breakfast, in summer at least, is outside in a small piazza. Rooms are all en suite and have air conditioning, safes, fridges and satellite TV. Low season prices are half those in high season.

D **Trento**, corso Porta Nuova 36, **T** 045 596444, **F** 045 591208, *Map 1, F4, p250* Halfway between the station and piazza Bra, Albergo Trento is a tired hotel surviving mainly on its relatively good value prices. There are a few balconies with geraniums, and rooms are simple with tiled floors and few frills. The decor is from the 'Fawlty Towers' school of design, and service is not much better either. It is, however, only 400 m from the Arena, and should you need a not-too-exorbitant place to collapse after a long night at the opera, it might be worth considering.

D Trieste, corso Porta Nuova 57, **T** 045 596022, **F** 045 8003510, www.hotel-trieste.it *Map 1, G4, p250* Less interesting than the hotel Verona next door, the hotel Trieste is nevertheless a better option than you might expect from its ugly, grey-concrete exterior. There are balconies facing corso Porta Nuova, and though the decor is plain, it is also reasonably warm and homely in style, as well as being sound-proofed and equipped with air conditioning, safes and en-suite bathrooms.

D Valverde, via Valverde 91, **T** 045 8033611, **F** 045 8031267. *Map 1, F3, p250* With some trees and even a café or two around, this end of via Valverde, in a generally unpromising area, is not unpleasant, though the hotel Valverde is an ugly square concrete building. Renovated in 2001, the rooms are decorated in supposedly Arte Povera style, all have air-conditioning and en suite bathrooms and some have balconies.

E Al Castello, corso Cavour 43, **T** 045 8004403. *Map 2, I2, p252* On a narrow road off corso Cavour, Al Castello is a small family-run hotel and restaurant with only ten rooms. The place as a whole has a slightly cluttered, homely feel, though rooms are fairly large, with carpets on wooden floors and some comfortable antiques.

E Armando, via Dietro Pallone 1, **T** 045 8000206, **F** 045 8036015. *Breakfast €8. Map 2, K6, p252* In an attractive, quiet area between piazza Bra and Ponte Aleardi, hotel Armando is plain but comfortable, and much better value than all the hotels further south. All 20 rooms have en-suite bathrooms, there is some decent art on the white walls alongside some old photos, and service is friendly. It's also next door to the good *Trattoria al Bersagliere*.

E Ciopeta, vicolo Teatro Filarmonico 2, **T** 045 8006843,
F 045 8033722, www.ciopeta.it *Map 2, J1, p252* Currently a small
and friendly, if simple, eight-room pension above a good restaurant,
there are plans afoot to refurbish and extend the Ciopeta, perhaps in
time for summer 2004. Prices, presumably, would also rise, however.

F Arena, Stradone Porta Palio 2, **T/F** 045 8032440. *Map 1, E4, p250*
In some ways more basic than the youth hostel, and certainly uglier,
the threadbare Arena has very little going for it except that it is
cheap and central. No credit cards, no breakfast, no entry after 0100
(except during the opera when the rule is extended to be "one hour
after the opera finishes") and no extras or luxuries of any kind. The
building itself is a brutal concrete lump, but it is at least set back from
the road in a courtyard, and is very near Castelvecchio. Rooms
without en-suite facilities are even cheaper than the rest.

Apartments

C Residence San Zeno, Regaste San Zeno 3, **T** 045 597721,
F 045 8002439, www.residencesanzenoverona.it/ *Map 1, E3, p250*
Residence San Zeno, near to Castelvecchio, is built on the ruins of
the Benedictine monastery of San Giovanni Alla Bevera, destroyed
in a 1492 flood. The present-day building has been well restored,
with lots of greenery cloaking the walls and a pergola, which
grows organic grapes for the buffet breakfast as well as shading
the courtyard. Irregular wooden beams, an eclectic collection of
antiques and worm-eaten tables give the place a homely feel. Each
room or apartment is individual – styles range from antique
through Liberty to plainer modern, and rooms vary in size from
singles to grand suites with kitchens and sitting rooms. Prices vary
markedly, too. The only downside may be the snooty and
unwelcoming attitude of the owner.

North and east of the Adige

Hostels

G Ostello della Gioventù Villa Francescatti, 15 Salita Fontana del Ferro, **T** 045 590360, **F** 045 8009127. *Up the hill behind the Teatro Romano. Bus 73 goes nearby every half an hour or so from the station, but it may be more convenient to get the frequent 11, 12, 13 or 14 (91-92 at weekends) to Ponte Navi and walk the last 15 mins or so. Open 0700-2330, breakfast 0730-0900, rooms closed 0900-1700, lights out 0000. Late return allowed for opera-goers. €12.50 per night including breakfast. Dinner €7.50, vegetarian meals only on request. Map 2, C8, p252* An old-fashioned hostel in an impressively grand old ex-monastery on the hillside above the city, Verona's youth hostel makes almost no concessions to modernity, but does what it does fairly well, and admirably cheaply. Comments in the visitors' book complain about "medieval" bureaucracy, but while the curfew and closing hours are a pain, and breakfast is a prison-like experience, the place is clean, attractive and generally efficient. There are 240 beds, all in single-sex dorms, although six rooms can be used by families ("but only families, no couples or groups of friends"). A spill-over building on via Santa Chiara (number 10, down the hill, nearer the river and slightly more modern) holds another 72. Bathrooms are clean and tiled, and there are pleasant gardens where guests can sit even when rooms are closed, but there's little, if any, privacy available. Information on notice boards can be out of date.

Apartments

E L'Ospite, via XX Settembre, 3, **T/F** 045 8036994, www.lospite.com *Map 2, B7, p252* Owner Federica De Rossi has

Sleeping

rooms and flats ranging from singles to flats equipped for four people. The position, next to the bridge of Ponte Navi, is excellent for both the sights of the *centro storico* across the river and the restaurants and bars of surrounding Veronetta. Prices drop for stays of a week or more.

Campsites

Campeggio Castel San Pietro, via Castel San Pietro 2, **T/F** 045 592037, www.campingcastelsanpietro.com *15 May-15 Oct. Office daily 0800-2300. € 5.50 per person, € 5-7 per plot, € 17-21 to hire one of two caravans. € 4-5 to rent a tent. Walk up the hill from Ponte Pietra and from Castel San Pietro follow the road around to the left. Map 2, B8, p252* Verona's campsite is extraordinarily well positioned, on the hill of San Pietro high above the *centro storico* with great views down through greenery to the city below. The campsite was started around 100 years ago by a botanist, and the 100 terraced plots are still home to more than 300 different varieties of plants. Staff are helpful and welcoming, speak good English, and even if you arrive in the early hours of the morning there is a sign telling you to find a plot and check in when you wake up. A small bar and shop sells essentials, there is a games room, and some of the small, dusty, vine-shaded placements are surrounded by 16th-century Venetian walls, the remains of ancient hill fortifications.

Lago di Garda

In some of the towns around the lake a sizeable proportion of accommodation is pre-booked by package holidays. Of the places easily accessible from Verona, Torri del Benaco is the most picturesque, Malcesine is also attractive and is good for access to the high slopes of Monte Baldo, while Torbole is the best option for watersports. Note that prices around the lake are usually quoted per person per night. Even when doubled, however, they are usually better value than in Verona.

Torri del Benaco

Hotels

D Gardesana, piazza Calderini 20, **T** 045 7225411, **F** 045 7225771, www.hotel-gardesana.com Dominating one side of Torri's ancient harbour, the Gardesana is in a building erected by the Venetians in 1452. 20th-century guests included Churchill, Lawrence Olivier, and King Juan Carlos I of Spain. All of this might lead you to expect higher prices, but even rooms with a balcony and lake view are very reasonable. Rooms are simple but classy 18th-century Venetian in style, with heavy antique furniture, en-suite bathrooms, air-conditioning and satellite TV. There is a buffet breakfast.

F Onda, via per Albisano, **T/F** 045 7225895. A few minutes walk east of the old town centre, the Onda is an exceptionally friendly place with an excellent buffet breakfast. Plain modern rooms, all with balconies, mostly look directly out over the lake. Very good value but no credit cards.

Malcesine

Hotels

F Casa Popi, via Gardesana 28, **T** 045 7400545, **F** 045 7401892, www.casapopi.com Towards the northern end of the town, near the cable car but away from the old centre, Casa Popi has a pool and garden. Modern but family-run, rooms are plain, though some have balconies with semi-obscured lake views.

F Dolomiti, via Monti 1, **T** 045 7400084, **F** 045 6583189, www.dolomitihotel.net An attractive hotel above a restaurant, the Dolomiti has en-suite rooms, all with modern facilities including satellite TV and air-conditioning. There is also an outside terrace and a bar.

Torbole

Hotels

D Benaco, via Benaco 18, **T** 0464 505364, **F** 0464 505973, www.onbenaco.com Right on the harbourfront in Torbole, a mere 50 m from the beach and 100 m from the ferry landing stage, the hotel Benaco, is as central as you can get, and has modern, well-equipped rooms and a generous buffet breakfast. There is also a free garage for mountain bikes and windsurfers.

E Casa Nataly, piazza Alpini 10, **T** 0464 505341, **F** 0464 506223, casanataly@tin.it On a quiet piazza, with geranium-entwined balconies, Nataly is a reliable, good-value option in a good position, with easy access to the waterfront.

Valpolicella and Lessinia

Valpolicella has few good hotels, but some excellent agriturismo options, which, as long as you have your own transport, would make good bases from which to tour the region. See www.agriturismoverona.it for more details.

The hills of Lessinia are also not overflowing with hotel options, but if you're walking through the area you might be interested in the basic but extraordinarily situated rifugi, which are a type of bunk barn, often with little or no facilities, but which provide a welcome roof, resting place, and often social meeting point during treks across the mountains. Rifugi are marked on walking maps of the area, or details can be found from the local tourist information or from www.prealpiveronesi.it/rifugi.htm

Hotels

F Lessinia, Piazzetta Alpini 2, Bosco Chiesanuova, **T** 045 6780151, **F** 045 6780098, www.hotellessinia.it   A fairly basic, but good value three-star hotel in Lessinia's biggest town. Hotel Lessinia is open all year round and has a private garage. Rooms are alpine in style and there is also a restaurant and *gelateria* attached.

Agriturismo

F Biotto, via Ca' de la Pela, Sant'Ambrogio di Valpolicella, **T** 045 7701505, **F** 045 7702681. *Rooms open Easter-mid-Sep. Restaurant open all year round. Restaurant: Thu-Sun 1200-1400, 1900-2200.*   Biotto is situated on the hills overlooking Sant'Ambrogio and has a great view all the way to Lake Garda. Traditional farmhouse style extends to the restaurant which in summer seats up to 40 people on the terrace outside and serves local dishes such as lasagne with rabbit. There are only two bedrooms, so booking ahead is advised, especially in high summer.

F Torre della Grola, via Zane 8, Sant'Ambrogio di Valpolicella, **T** 045 7732444, **F** 045 6884401. *Open all year round. Restaurant Thu-Sun 1200-1400, 2000-2200.*   In an attractive 18th-century building with wooden floors, olive trees, stone walls, wooden beams and a crenellated tower, Torre della Grola is a restored farmhouse with seven bedrooms with en-suite bathrooms. Traditional food in the restaurant includes risotto made with amarone and roasted rabbit.

Vicenza

Hotels

E-F Albergo Due Mori, contrà Do Rode 26, **T** 0444 321886,
F 0444 326127. *Breakfast €5 per person. Map 3, E5, p254*
Kitted out smartly in early 20th-century style, and with an
attractive exterior, Due Mori is quiet and spacious, as well as
being very well placed for the centre of Vicenza. A couple of
double rooms with balconies are especially desirable, but may
need to be fought for. Two rooms on the ground floor are
equipped for disabled visitors.

F Vicenza, stradella dei Nodari, **T** 0444 321512.
Map 3, D5, p254 An ex-theatre, the Vicenza is a stone's throw from
piazza dei Signori and has an ageing charm: comfortable but
slightly ragged around the edges. Many rooms have balconies over
the quiet street below, and all have small en-suite bathrooms.

Mantova

Hotels

D Broletto, via Accademia 1, **T** 0376 326784, **F** 0376 221297.
Breakfast €5 per person. Map 4, E6, p255 With only sixteen rooms
in a smart building the Broletto is cosy and homely and fills up
quickly in the summer. Balconies have geraniums growing, rooms
have big beds and some have wooden-beamed ceilings.

D Due Guerreri, piazza Sordello 52, **T** 0376 321533,
F 0376 329645. *Map 4, D6, p255* Very central, just off the southern
edge of piazza Sordello, Due Guerreri has 30 fairly plain rooms,
some with views over the piazza. Tiled and cool (with

Despite being a wealthy, smart city, Verona has a tradition for small family-run *trattorie* and *osterie* which it is very proud of, so much so that even some of its smartest and most expensive restaurants like to call themselves *Trattoria* this, or *Osteria* that. In theory *osterie* are primarily places for drinking, whereas *trattorie* concentrate on food, but don't read too much into names. Veronese cuisine, showing influences from north of the Alps, is mostly rich and heavy, with large quantities of polenta and horsemeat on most menus. Bigoli, a sort of thick spaghetti, is the most common type of pasta, and pearà (a sauce made of bone marrow, bread and pepper) is, supposedly, a Veronese delicacy. A full meal will consist of a starter (antipasto), a first course (usually pasta) and a second (usually meat or fish). Nobody will object if you choose only one or two parts of this, however. It's normal to drink wine with a meal. Pizzas are not a local tradition, and it's worth shopping around for a good one. Local produce you might find on menus includes kiwi fruit, radicchio, melons and chestnuts.

€ **Eating codes**

€€€€	€24 and over
€€€	€18-24
€€	€14-18
€	€14 and under

Prices refer to an average two-course meal without drinks. You can eat more cheaply by just having a first course, often pasta.

Centro storico

Restaurants

€€€€ **Ristorante Maffei**, piazza Erbe 38, **T** 045 8010015, **F** 045 8005124, www.ristorantemaffei.it *Mon-Sun 1200-1400, 1900-2200. Map 2, F5, p252* Probably the smartest restaurant in Verona, Maffei is in the Casa Maffei itself, at the top of piazza Erbe, on the spot where the Roman Capitol once stood. The best tables are outside in the courtyard under large pillars. First courses include farfalle with vegetables, and sausage and pappardelle with porcini mushrooms, while for second course there are cheese, fish and meat options, such as taleggio with pear, bass baked in a potato crust, and pork with dijon mustard and green apple. The mouthwatering six-course "Menu degustazione Torre dei Lamberti" is €65 per person.

€€€ **Hostaria del Sole**, via Garibaldi 16/a, **T** 045 8008261. *Mon, Wed-Sun 1230-1430, 1930-2230. Map 2, E5, p252* An *osteria* with pretensions to greater things, del Sole offers innovative dishes such as guinea fowl with black olive and onion sauce and ravioli with chicory and cheese alongside the more standard, such as rocket and tuna fish salad.

Local wines

Amarone is similar in the process of production to Recioto, except that fermentation is stopped earlier and Amarone then undergoes a five-year ageing. It is the most recent wine of the Valpolicella group, having only been made since after World War Two. Dry and intense rather than sweet it is probably the area's best wine, but is also very expensive. It is used to make the eponymous risotto found in many of Verona's restaurants.

Bardolino Cultivated on the shores of Lake Garda, Bardolino is a dry fruity red. It uses the same three grapes as Valpolicella but with the addition of Negrara. there is also a rosé version, (the pink colour is a result of a shorter fermentation period) which is often drunk as an aperitivo.

Custoza A dry white with almond tones from south of Lake Garda, this wine is made from six varieties of grape and has an alcohol content of less than 11%.

Recioto Valpolicella The rece, or ears, are the outer grapes of bunches, which are left to dry before being used to make this rich, sweet wine which dates back to ancient Roman times.

Soave From the hills around Soave, to the east of Verona, comes this fresh white, made from Garganega and Trebbiano grapes. Recioto Soave is a richer, sweeter version made using a similar process to that of Recioto Valpolicella (see below).

Valdadige Upstream from Verona, partly into the province of Trentino, this young, fresh, fruity wine comes in both red and white varieties.

Valpolicella The area's best-known wine, from a large area to the west of Verona between the Negrar and Adige valleys, suffers from a somewhat unfair reputation for quaffability above quality. Especially in its Classico and Superiore versions, Valpolicella can be a fine, rich, smooth wine. Classico comes only from the most traditional Valpolicella area, while Superiore is aged for at least a year. The wine is made from Corvina, Rondinella and Molinara grapes.

€€€ **La Toretta**, piazza Broilo 1, **T** 045 8010099,
www.latorrettaristorante.it Mon-Sat 1200-1500, 1900-2300
(1830-2300 on opera nights). *Map 2, C6, p252* A smart restaurant
halfway between the Duomo and Ponte Pietra, La Toretta offers a
few embellishments to the traditional Veronese menu with
antipasti such as tartlets of courgette and speck with a taleggio
sauce, a *fantasia di verdure* (vegetable fantasy) and good though
pricey gnocchi and risotto. There is a profusion of greenery around
the door and there are quiet tables outside.

€€€ **Ristorante al Cristo**, piazzetta Pescheria 6,
T 045 594287. *Tue-Sun 1100-1500, 1800-0100.* *Map 2, F6, p252*
In the quiet and beautiful piazzetta Pescheria, site of the medieval
fish market, this smart restaurant has an attractive covered
outdoor seating area, good service and a relatively good-value
menù fisso for €16 consisting of a first course of salad, ham,
mozzarella or oysters followed by grilled chicken or salmon and a
side-dish. Other dishes include tuna fillet with olives and capers,
spinach gnocchi with polenta and baccalà with polenta.

€€€ **VeronAntica**, via Sottoriva 10a, **T** 045 8004124.
*1000-1530, 1800-0100, kitchen 1200-1430, 1915-2245 (on opera
days, 1830-2245).* *Map 2, F7, p252* VeronAntica has tables
outside in vicolo Rigaste Orti and a couple of rooms sunk down
inside, and is one of the smarter places on via Sottoriva to eat.
Good pasta dishes include tagliatelle with almond pesto and
there is a good choice of fish dishes for second course, too, such
as grilled trout, or fish 'al brandy'. For the full works, splash out
on a menu VeronAntica for €28.50.

€€ **Giulietta e Romeo**, corso Sant'Anastasia 27,
T 045 8009177. *Mon 1830-2230, Tue-Sun 1215-1430.*
Map 2, E6, p252 This traditional *osteria* has an extensive wine list
and an excellent selection of local dishes, including good

★ Cheap eats

pappardelle e pomodorini, and polenta with just about everything. The lower part of the restaurant is an old wine cellar and still has a brick barrel-vaulted ceiling. The management is the same as the *Osteria Al Duca* in via Arche nearby. The set lunch *menù* consists of a first and a second course for €13.

€€ **Hostaria la Vecchia Fontanina**, piazzetta Chiavica 5, **T** 045 591159. *Mon-Sat 1200-1430, 1930-2230.*
Map 2, F7, p252 In a quiet nook off Santa Maria in Chiavica, not far from piazza dei Signori, with a parasol-shaded outdoor seating area, this attractive little restaurant attracts a mixed crowd of mainly Italians. Highlights of a varied and interesting menu include bigoli (pasta) with nettles and smoked cheese, polenta with various toppings, and ostrich. Even the bread and the house wine are a cut above the average.

€€ **Osteria Al Duca**, via Arche Scaligeri 2, **T** 045 594474.
Summer, Mon-Fri 1200-1430, 1800-2230, Sat 1200-1430, winter, Mon, Wed-Sat, 1200-1430, 1830-2230. Map 2, F6, p252 In the supposed Casa di Romeo (Romeo's house), Al Duca is an excellent little restaurant with a wine list longer than your arm, with no fewer than 22 types of Amarone. At times its popularity is too much for its own good – if you're forced to sit upstairs in a plain room and suffer stressed and hurried service, you may not fully appreciate its charms. Downstairs, however, it's one of the city's most attractive restaurants, dark, atmospheric and full of character. The food is excellent too,

with plenty of tasty pasta choices followed by some meaty second courses. The set lunch *menù*, as in its sister restaurant *Giulietta e Romeo* (see above), consists of a first and a second course for €13.

€€ **Osteria Le Vecete**, via Pellicciai 32, **T** 045 594748. *0900-0200, closed Sun except in high summer. Stays open after opera. Map 2, G5, p252* Right in the centre but on a relatively quiet road, friendly Le Vecete has very amenable opening hours, and, in an atmospheric, wood-beamed setting, offers a good selection of wine and food and some laid-back tunes. First courses include pasta salad, lasagne and pasta with swordfish and cherry tomatoes. Meaty main courses are also available. There are good *panini* and *foccacia* available throughout the day and good *Theresianer* beer on tap.

€€ **Osteria Trattoria Al Duomo**, via Duomo 7a, **T** 045 8004505. *Mon-Sat 1100-1500, 1800-0000, kitchen 1200-1430, 1930-2230. Map 2, D6, p252* The small, atmospheric Al Duomo is one of the city's best *trattorie*. With a bar, small wooden tables, beams and bricks, old photos and antique instruments on the walls, the only thing which detracts from the atmosphere is the likes of the Communards and Bon Jovi coming from the stereo. Service can be erratic too, but the excellent food makes up for this. Tasty dishes are prepared with obvious care and attention. The ravioli with spinach and smoked ricotta is especially good, as is the swordfish with rocket and cherry tomatoes, and prices are very reasonable. The double billing as *osteria trattoria* means you can stay and drink after you've finished eating.

€€ **Taverna di via Stella**, via Stella 5c, **T** 045 8008008. *Tue-Sun 1030-1430, 1800-2300. Map 2, G6, p252* Billing itself as an '*Osteria con cucina*', the Taverna di via Stella is actually more a restaurant with a bar attached. The walls have non-antique frescoes, designed to look as if they are flaking, but it manages to be a reasonably atmospheric place despite this. There is a blue-painted ceiling with stars (a reference to the name) and wooden benches and chairs. The wine list is good, and extensive, and there is a wide selection of polenta dishes. Service can be a little cocksure, but the excellent home-made desserts make up for it.

€ **Carro Armato**, vicolo Gatto 2a, **T** 045 8030175. *Mon and Tue, Thu-Sat 1100-0200, Sun 1100-0000. Map 2, E2, p252* Generally considered a night-spot (see p166), Carro Armato also does extremely good local dishes. The pasta choices are especially good, but there are also meat and fish second course choices, and home-made desserts. All of which should be washed down with a bottle or two from the enormous wine list, of course.

€ **Pizzeria Vesuvio**, 20 corso Sant'Anastasia, **T** 045 595460. *Tue-Sun 1130-1500, 1800-2230. Map 2, F5, p252* This small pizzeria near piazza Erbe has a cramped but sociable upstairs room, with wooden beams and air-conditioning. Pizzas have good authentically crisp-yet-chewy bases though they are a little on the small side. There is a ridiculously large choice of toppings, some of which are less than traditional. Despite the advertised 0100 closing time, the place is seldom open much beyond 2230.

€ **Trattoria alla Trota**, via Trota 3, **T** 045 8004757. *Mon-Sat 1200-1500, 1830-2230. Map 2, F7, p252* Old enough that the street is named after the restaurant rather than vice versa, and well known enough that the sign is a metal trout rather than the word, this small *trattoria* is a Veronese institution. The lunch *menù* is particularly good value at € 11 for a first of pasta or soup and a meaty second with vegetables, salad or fries. Other specialities include fettucine with artichokes and penne Mexicana (pasta with cream, chillies and sausage). Service and decor is, like the food, fairly simple.

★ **Cafés**

Best

• Caffè alle Fogge, p141.
• Cappa Café, p166.
• Caffè Tubino, p142.
• Puntogi, p142.
• Pasticceria Barini, p148.

Cafés

Caffè alle Fogge, via Fogge 10, **T** 045 8006831. *Mon-Tue 0830-2200, Wed-Sun 0830-2400. Sep-May closed Tue. Map 2, F5, p252* Under the northern arch of piazza dei Signori a small street leads up to this friendly café with good bar snacks. In the middle of the day this is also a good spot for a light lunch, with a *menù* of a pasta dish, a dessert and a drink for €15. It's also not bad for freshly-made sandwiches. At night it livens up considerably, with the narrow line of outside tables usually full.

Caffè Rialto, via Diaz 2, **T** 045 8012845. *Mon-Sun 0730-0100 Map 2, G4, p252* In the shadow of Porta Borsari (see p52), this café has its own piece of *pavimento romano* under glass in the floor in front of the bar. A plaque on the wall outside marks the peak of the 1868 flood. Alongside a good selection of drinks there are two strangely incongruous posters of golfers on the wall.

Bar della Libreria, Libreria Gheduzzi, corso Sant'Anastasia 7, **T** 045 8002234. *Daily 0900-2400. Map 2, F5, p252* At the back of this excellent bookshop (see p192) is a good meeting place, with art exhibitions and good salads.

Cappa Café, piazzetta Bra Molinari 1. *Daily 0800-0200. Map 2, D7, p252* Tardis-like, what appears to be a small café opens out into a cavernous interior in a Bohemian style and a small terrace right on the river, looking across at the Teatro Romano. Food is mainly simple but filling pasta dishes, and there is jazz on Sundays. The atmosphere, however, can feel tourist-orientated. See also p166.

Caffè Tubino, 15/d corso Porta Borsari, **T** 045 8032296. *Daily 0700-2300. Map 2, G4, p252* Excellent coffee and *cornetti* are served in this distinctive little café, stacked high with coffee- and tea-related paraphernalia from around the world. The range of teas available is unusually big, and you can buy both coffee beans and tea leaves to take away.

Crestanello, via Ponte Nuovo 8/a, **T** 045 8032226. *Mon-Fri 0730-0000, Sat and Sun 0830-0000. Map 2, G8, p252* A smart, airy, modern café with a good choice of speciality coffees as well as ice-creams and posh sandwiches.

Puntogi, via Ponte Nuovo 9d, **T** 045 8009125. *Mon-Sat 1000-0200, Sun 1700-0200. Map 2, G8, p252* On a corner next to the river near the end of via Sottoriva, Puntogi has an excellent outside seating area and is open late every night. A great place from which to watch the world go by.

Gelaterias

Balù, 57b corso Porta Borsari, **T** 045 8036341. *Map 2, G4, p252* In the shadow of Porta Borsari, queues regularly form for the excellent ice-creams from this modern gelateria. The chocolate is especially dark and the panna cotta is unusually rich and tasty. There is another branch at 1/c via Roma.

Orchidea, piazza Erbe 22, **T** 045 591512. *Mon, Wed-Sun 0800-2400. Map 2, G6, p252* The best ice-creams on Verona's

★ **Best**

Gelaterias

- Pampanin, p143.
- Balù, p142.
- Ponte Pietra, p143.
- Bonvicini, p148.
- Ponte della Vittoria, p149.

central piazzas come from this unassuming little café beside the Arco della Costa, leading into piazza dei Signori.

Pampanin, via Garibaldi 24, **T** 045 8030064. *Mon, Wed-Fri 0730-0000, Sat and Sun 0730-1300, 1530-0000. Map 2, D4, p252* Just over Ponte Garibaldi into the *centro storico*, Pampanin's *gelati* are considered by many to be the city's best. The selection is neither enormous nor especially inventive, but what they do they do mouth-wateringly well.

Ponte Pietra, via Ponte Pietra 23. *Mon 1530-2000, Tue-Sun 1100-2200. Map 2, C6, p252* Excellent home-made ice-cream with which to wander across the bridge.

South of the centro storico

Restaurants

€€€€ **Trattoria Tre Marchetti**, vicolo Tre Marchetti 19B, **T** 045 8030463. *Sep-Jun closed Sun, Mon open evenings only, Jul and Aug closed Mon. Map 2, I4, p252* Almost within touching distance of the Arena and catering to peckish opera-goers both before and after the show, Tre Marchetti is a smart sophisticated take on the *trattoria* tradition. Two lines of immaculate tables sit in a frescoed interior on which are served delicacies such as 'medaglions of aromatized rabbit' and mashed potato with truffles. The *menu a degustazione* costs €60 a head. Booking necessary before and after opera.

€€€€ Tre Corone, piazza Bra, **T** 045 8002462. *Tue-Sun 1230-1400, 1830-2200, also after opera. Map 2, J3, p252* If you want to sit out on the Listone of piazza Bra itself, this is the best option, though not the cheapest. Food is good, if fairly simple, given the high prices, and service is attentive. Firsts include ravioli with mascarpone and peas with butter and parmesan. Seconds include grilled beef with parsley and courgettes, and fresh tuna fish with french beans, olive oil and sun-dried tomatoes.

€€€ Le Cantine de L'Arena, piazzetta Scalette Rubiani 1, **T** 045 8032849, **F** 045 8026373. *Daily 1200-0100 during opera season, otherwise daily 1200-1500, 1900-2300. Map 2, I4, p252* Possibly the best of the piazza Bra tourist traps, Le Cantine is actually set back on an adjoining piazzetta, but is no more than a stone's throw from the walls of the Arena. As well as fairly good pizzas, the restaurant has a kitchen which rustles up traditional Italian and Veronese dishes. Waiters play heavily on their Italian panache and swagger, but are also very helpful and eager to please.

€€ Al Bersagliere, via Dietro Pallone 1, **T** 045 8004824, **F** 045 8004932, trattoriabersagliere@inwind.it *Mon-Sat 1200-1430, 1930-2200, also open as a bar from 0800 Map 2, L6, p252* Specializing in traditional Veronese and Lessinian food, Al Bersagliere has plenty of polenta-based dishes as well as smoked goose breast, trout with soave wine (which comes under the heading "other curiously things") and lots of wine and home-made desserts. There is a small garden, a bar with wooden tables and a friendly Italian atmosphere.

€€ Al Calmiere, piazza San Zeno 10, **T** 045 8030765, **F**045 8031900, www.calmiere.com *Wed 1230-1430, Fri-Tue 1230-1430, 2000-2230. Map 1, D2, p250* In a shady position right on

Eating and drinking

▶ **Golden bread**

Pandoro literally means *gold bread* (pan d'oro). The tall, star-shaped cake, sprinkled with vanilla icing sugar, is a Veronese Christmas tradition which is increasingly found all over the world. Probably dating from the kitchens of the Venetian aristocracy in the 18th century, it combines the local star shape of Nadalin, another Christmas cake, with the risen style of Vienna which was fashionable at the time. Bauli started industrial production of the cakes in the 1950s in Verona, and now also make all sorts of variations, including panettone (pandoro with dried fruit) filled with cointreau cream, and Colomba, an Easter cake, with almonds and candied fruit. The company now employs around 660 people and produces 31,000 tons of cake a year.

piazza San Zeno, with a view of the church doors through the trees, Al Calmiere is a friendly, taverna-like place in a 15th-century building with lots of wood, Tiffany glass screens, a large fireplace, a barrel, window boxes and a good, if exceptionally meaty, menu. Antipasti include bresaola with goats' cheese and rocket salad, firsts include handmade bigoli with a choice of sauces and seconds include veal with tuna and capers. Home-made desserts include a tiramisù made with pandoro. The wine list extends to over 400 local labels.

€€ **Da Urbano**, piazza Corrubio 29, **T** 045 8032997. *Mon, Wed-Sun 1030-1500, 1730-0100. Map 1, E2, p250* A pizzeria and restaurant near San Zeno, Da Urbano has shaded tables outside and specializes in Sardinian dishes, including ravioli with tomatoes and pecorino cheese and gnochetti alla campidanese – pasta with tomatoes, Sardinian sausage, fennel seeds and parsley. There is also a fish menu and both "special" and "super" pizzas.

A street named desire

As well as Juliet's house, via Cappello has some of Verona's busiest shops, cafés and restaurants.

€€ **Pam Pam**, corso Porta Borsari 55, **T** 045 8030363. *Daily 1200-1430, 1800-2300. Map 2, G4, p252* Not the cheapest pizzas around, but some of the best, cooked in a traditional wood oven within stretching distance of Porta Borsari. There is also a pasta menu, with traditional dishes, but most come for the pizzas.

€€ **Trattoria a Lanterna**, corso Porta Nuova 46a, **T** 045 595254. *Daily 1200-1430, 1900-2230. Bookings also taken for after opera. Map 1, G4, p251* This *trattoria* specializes in Sicilian food and does good pasta/fresh fish and fresh shellfish combinations, such as *taglierini con vongole* as well as risottos and delicious fishy first courses.

€€ **Trattoria Portichetti**, piazza Portichetti 6, **T** 045 8032364. *Mon-Sat 1200-1430, 1930-2230. Map 1, D3, p250* This friendly, simple *trattoria* near San Zeno has traditional Veronese dishes and a good-value *pranzo di lavoro* (working lunch) set menu of a first course, a second course, a side dish, a quarter of wine and half a litre of water for €11, Monday to Friday lunchtimes only. Neither the menu, or the small, stark, rectangular setting offer much in the way of frills.

€ **Osteria Casa Vino**, vicolo Morette 8, **T** 045 8004337. *1230-1430, 1930-2230, closed Mon in summer, Sun in winter. Map 2, J1, p252* Between Castelvecchio and piazza Bra, this good value *osteria* has a few umbrella-shaded tables outside in a quiet street, and offers friendly service and potted plants. First courses, all €5, include tagliatelle with rabbit, macaroni with vegetables and smoked ricotta, and gnocchi with pecorino cheese and chicory. Second courses include duck with spinach and onions, and baccalà with polenta.

€ **Pizzeria Trattoria Bella Napoli**, via G marconi 16, **T** 045 591143. *Tue-Sun, 1200-1420, 1830-0030. Map 1, F4, p250* Verona's best pizzas, as is only right, come from a restaurant which replicates just about everything about the city that invented them, Naples. From the bases and toppings to the humour and the opening hours, just about everything here is sturdily Neapolitan, and (humour aside) reliably excellent. Pizzas are available by the metre as well as in the more traditional rounds. As a guide, half a metre is about right for two people with good appetites. You may have to wait for a table at the busiest times. On these occasions make sure you give your name to the waiter when you arrive.

€ **Pizzeria Trattoria Ponte Navi**, via Dogana 1/a, **T** 045 591203. *Mon-Wed, Fri-Sun, pizzas 1200-1500, 1800-0000, trattoria 1200-1430, 1830-2230. Map 2, I7, p252* With two levels of terrace

★ **Drinking holes**

ⓑⓔⓢⓣ
・Carro Armato, p166.
・Sottoriva 23, p167.
・Osteria Sottoriva, p166.
・Square, p167.
・Al Mascaron, p168.

outside, one beside the river, this is a good place to eat outside in the summer. The pizzas themselves are the culinary highlight, though the choice of around seventy varieties may be a little overwhelming. There is a lunchtime set menu with traditional home-made dishes.

Cafés

Du de Spade, piazza Corrubio 2. *Mon-Wed, Sat 0745-2055, Thu 0715-2055. Map 1, E2, p250* A no-nonsense café near to San Zeno with an excellent selection of sandwiches and plenty of character. Popular with older locals.

Pasticceria Barini, 8 corso Porta Nuova, **T** 045 8030449, www.pasticceriabarini.it *Mon-Sat 0630-2030. Map 2, K2, p252* An unusually good selection of cakes and pastries makes Barini, just south of piazza Bra, an especially good place for a morning coffee. It's also a good place to buy sweet delicacies to be boxed up and taken home.

Gelaterias

Bonvicini, vicolo Ghiaia 5a, **T** 045 8000148. *Mon-Tue, Thu-Sat 1030-2330. Map 2, K3, p252* An excellent range of flavours is made on the premises and sold in industrial quantities to locals who come to this hidden-away gelateria, on a road off corso Porta

Nuova, to buy it in boxes. There are also cups and cones available, however, and as well as Sicilian granita, ice-cream flavours include fig and grapefruit. There is even a range of soya ice-cream.

Ponte della Vittoria, via Diaz 8. **T** 045 8004276. *Daily 0630-0000*. Delicious home-made ice-creams with plenty of flavour available at all hours of the day from near Porta Borsari. And at only €0.80 a scoop, a veritable bargain.

North and east of the Adige

Restaurants

€€€ **Ristorante ai Teatri**, via Santa Maria Rocca Maggiore 8, **T** 045 8012181, www.ristoranteaiteatri.it *Mon 1900-2300, Tue-Sat 1230-1430, 1900-2300. Map 2, F8, p252* Specialities of this smart restaurant near the river include stuffed tomatoes with radicchio in aubergine sauce, cream of asparagus with clams and thyme, and pork with honey and grilled potato mille-feuille.

€€ **Osteria Trattoria Perbacco**, 48 via G Carducci, **T** 045 594193. *Mon-Sat 1230-1430, 1930-2230. Map 1, D7, p250* Laid-back contemporary music, wooden tables and panelling, lights hung with coloured veils and a verdant rear courtyard all set the scene for this excellent and good-value *trattoria*. Authentic Veronese cuisine with some imaginative variations is served in a young and friendly atmosphere, students mixing with professionals. Daily specials can be delicious and regulars

! Cultivation of kiwi fruit in the Veneto region contributes to Italy being the world's biggest producer of kiwis. The hairless 'Top Star' variety was discovered by a Veronese farmer.

such as pasta with goats cheese, rucola and hazelnuts, and polenta with cheese, smoked lardo (a kind of coarse pâté) and mushrooms are highly recommended. Even the bread and house wine are good. English is spoken, but not so much as to detract from the authentic local feel.

€€ **Ristorante Pizzeria Redentore**, via Redentore 15/17, **T** 045 8005932. *Tue 1900-0000, Wed-Sun 1200-1430. Map 2, C8, p252* On the point of the junction of via Redentore and Lungadige Re Teodorico, between the river and the Teatro Romano, Redentore has an umbrella-shaded seating area with good views in either direction. Portions of pasta are big, especially the spaghetti with seafood which is easily big enough to be a whole meal. There are unusually good vegetarian options for both first and second courses, including a generous plate of grilled vegetables with mozzarella. Pizzas, fish dishes and salads are also all good, but desserts tend to be too sweet and sickly. There is also a large air-conditioned indoor space.

€€ **Trattoria alla Isolo**, 5 piazza Isolo. *Map 2, G8, p252* This small and friendly, but slightly basic, *trattoria* has the feeling of being in someone's house. In fact it's quite possible that various members of the family will sit on one of the other four or five tables eating, talking and watching television over your head. The food is simple traditional Veneto home cooking: pasta with truffles, gnocchi, baccalà and some good dense cakes.

€€ **Trattoria da Ropeton**, 1 Fontana del Ferro, **T** 045 8030040. *Wed-Mon 1215-1430, 1930-2245 Map 1, B8, p250* In a quiet corner of the city, near the youth hostel, Ropeton is a *trattoria* often recommended by locals. It's a spacious, friendly place, with seats outside across the road, as well as the bright, peach tableclothed area inside. Simple first and second courses tend to be on the heavy side but are full of flavour. The tagliolini with

★ **Posh eats**

ω
ω
ω
ω
ω

•Ristorante Maffei, p135.
•Ristorante al Cristo, p137.
•VeronAntica, p137.
•Trattoria Tre Marchetti, p143.
•Ristorante ai Teatri, p149.

mascarpone, truffles, porcini mushrooms, hazelnuts and rocket is especially good. The penne al Ropeton is also held in high esteem but may be too rich and too reminiscent of English curry sauce for non-Italian palates. Second courses are very horsey. Home-made desserts are excellent, particularly the panna cotta.

€ **La Focacceria**, via XX Settembre 17, **T** 045 548350. *Mon-Fri 0930-2030, Sat 1430-2030. Map 2, I8, p252* You'll probably pay less than € 2 for a large, filling and tasty slice of freshly made focaccia at this friendly little place, popular with students. There's always a selection of toppings. Bottled beers and soft drinks are also available.

€ **La Vecchia Canna**, via Scrimiari 5, **T** 045 595956. *Mon-Fri 1000-1500, 1830-0200, Sat 1830-0200. Map 2, I8, p252* Exceptionally good value *menùs* mean this is a popular spot, especially at lunchtime. A small place, set down from the street, the atmosphere is that of a bar, but € 7.76 for a first course, second course, vegetables, wine and coffee pulls in the eaters as well as the drinkers.

€ **Locanda del Fiume**, 15/a via Santa Maria Rocca Maggiore, **T** 045 8007751. *Tue-Fri 1200-1430, 1900-0030, Sat and Sun 1900-0030. Map 2, F8, p252* Thirty different types of *bruschettone* (big bruschetta) are served in this bar-restaurant a street back from the river. Prices range from €3.50-5. There is also a selection of pasta dishes and salads as well as some good beers and wine.

€ **Ostaria la Stueta**, via Redentore 4b, **T** 045 8032462. *Map 2, D8, p252* Near the Teatro Romano, this small *osteria* does a good selection of traditional home-made Veronese fare. The setting is also firmly traditional, with wooden beams, tiled floor, wooden tables and white tablecloths. The fettucini with marsala wine and gorgonzola is especially tasty but the pasta fagioli (pasta with beans) is also unusually subtle and tasty. The second courses rely very heavily on freshly made polenta, with various choices including *baccalà* (salt cod), cuttlefish and *pastisada* (horse stew). Service is very attentive and the wine list is good.

€ **Pero D'Oro**, via Ponte Pignolo 25. *Near piazza del Isolo. Tue-Sun 1200-1400, 1930-2200. Map 2, E2, p252* This simple but traditional family-run place, tucked away on an anonymous side street, has a limited menu, but is good value. A choice of two set menus for €15 and €16 includes two courses, a side dish, wine and water. There are also a few other pasta and second course options. The *bigoli* (thick Veronese pasta) is good, second courses and salads are fairly standard, but vegetables are disappointingly soggy. Draped lampshades add a degree of atmosphere, and there are original, if derivative, paintings on the walls.

Lago di Garda

The fishy influences of the lake combine with the Germanic influences of tourist-pressure to produce an occasionally eclectic but usually tasty cuisine. Many of the lakeside restaurants cater to a lowest common denominator and can end up being bland. Search a bit further back from the waterfront, however, and the food is often good, often with excellent fish. Pizzas, too, are more reliably good than you might expect in such a tourist-orientated environment.

Torri del Benaco

Restaurants

€€€ Trattoria Bar Bell'Arrivo, piazza Calderini 10, **T** 045 6299028, **F** 045 6290256. *Tue-Sun 1200-1400, 1900-2200*. On the main lake road, Bell'Arrivo is slightly hidden away from the main tourist focus of the town, but is possibly its best restaurant. Tables outside under a plant-entwined pergola are a fine setting for the chef's choice dishes of trout salad with early vegetables or crêpes with ricotta and asparagus. Other highlights include lake pike and trout and grilled Monte Baldo cheese.

€€ Ristorante Pizzeria Alla Grotta, corso D Alighieri 57, **T** 045 7225839. *Daily 1200-1430, 1730-2230, Sep-May closed Tue*. Understandably the most popular part of this restaurant is a wooden platform built from the promenade out over the lake, which can be seen through slats below. Both seafood and pizzas are good, though some of the former is made using frozen rather than fresh lake fish. The atmosphere is vibrant and you may have to wait for an outside table.

€ Ristorante Pizzeria Da Carlo, piazza Umberto I, **T** 045 7225433. *Daily 1200-1400, 1800-2200, closed Oct-Mar*. With excellent pizzas on the piazza near the waterfront, Da Carlo is popular in the evening when you can watch the sunset over the mountains opposite. Should you be forced inside, the peach decor is an altogether less pleasant experience. There are also other non-pizza dishes available, but the fish selection is relatively meagre, and it's the pizzas most come for.

! It takes about 10 kg of grapes to make one bottle of Amarone, compared to around 1 kg for other red wines.

Cafés

Bar Gheo, via D Alighieri 22. Lots of Italians sit outside at this café bar, especially at aperitivo time when it's a good spot for people-watching, and when the snacks are also good. The small barrel-vaulted bar is hidden away under external stairs.

Malcesine

Restaurants

€€€ Ristorante Enosophia, via Navene 2, **T** 045 6584286, **F** 045 6583140, www.enosophia.it *Mon, Wed-Sun 1230-1330, 1930-2230.* A smart restaurant with wooden furniture, a courtyard and low-lit, barrel-vaulted rooms, Enosophia is perhaps more suited to supper than lunch. The menu has some innovative takes on traditional dishes: antipasti include marinated vegetables with coriander and white wine and spinach pudding with iced gazpacho. There are some interesting pasta dishes too, spaghetti with rabbit sauce and pasta with perch and tomato sauce. Second courses are primarily fishy and include steamed bass with crayfish sauce.

€€€ Taverna dei Capitani, corso Garibaldi 2, **T** 045 7400005. *Daily 1200-1400, 1830-2230.* One of Malcesine's oldest restaurants, the Taverna dei Capitani, on a quiet street near the centre of town, has a courtyard as well as its atmospheric wood-beamed interior with ancient sea paraphernalia. There are lots of pasta dishes, but fish is the real speciality with dishes such as ravioli with lake perch and melted butter.

€€ Caffè Porto Vecchio, piazza Magenta 8, **T** 045 6584335. *Daily 1200-1430, 1830-2230.* On Malcesine's most attractive square, with the lake lapping at the edge of the old port, this restaurant serves excellent food at outside tables away from the hum of bus tours. First courses include the excellent tagliolini with scallops and courgettes, second courses include fish kebabs and there are also good salads, such as rocket, mushrooms and parmesan. Outside of main mealtimes the place reverts to a café and sells sangria, mojitos, milkshakes and ice-cream.

Cafés

Hippopotamus Wine Bar, piazza Cavour, **T** 045 6570069. This fashionable bijou wine bar has two or three tables outside, and a sunken interior with a small bar and walls lined with bottles.

Gelaterias

Cento Per Cento, via Castello 31. Just outside the castle gates, this gelateria has an interesting selection of home-made ice-creams including a supposedly energy-giving ginseng flavour.

Torbole

Restaurants

€€ **Al Pescatore**, 11-13 viale Giovanni Segantini, **T** 0464 505236. *Daily Jun-Aug 1200-1500, Sep-May 1700-2400.* One of Torbole's least touristy eating places, Pescatore has, as the name suggests, a good range of fish and seafood, including smoked swordfish and local grilled trout. Also rucola and parmesan on offer and good pizzas, too. Inside it's a little cramped, but outside there are some simple white metal tables down a side-street.

€€ **Due Mollini**, piazza Benacense 4, **T** 0464 505383. *Daily 1200-1500, 1730-2400*. Sprawling, with benches and tables out the front under an awning, more tables inside and more still out the back. Serves enormous portions of basic pasta and pizzas. Quantity comes before quality, but it's a good place to sit on the piazza, and it should certainly fill you up after some hard windsurfing.

Cafés

Wind's Bar, via Matteotti 72, **T** 0464 505232. *Daily 0700-0200, Sep-Mar closed Tue*. With tables and seats made from snowboards and bike wheels, and with just about everything else shiny chrome, Wind's is a hip young bar going for the windsurfing market; which doesn't stop distinctly square, elderly Germans stopping by for pots of tea. Sandwiches, salads and snacks are also on offer.

Valpolicella and Lessinia

Restaurants

€€ **Bar Trattoria Valsorda**, Cascate di Mollina, Fumame, **T** 045 7701867. *Sat and Sun, Mon-Sun in high summer. Irregular hours*. A slightly eccentric bar, café and restaurant with a mix of passing day-trippers and sedentary locals, this makes a good starting and finishing place for trips up into the surrounding valleys. Traditional local food includes polenta and pasta.

€€ **Pizzeria Villa Renzi**, San Vito di Negrar, **T** 045 7501072. *Closed Wed*. In an extremely handsome old villa in Negrar, Pizzeria Villa Renzi does a wide range of excellent pizzas in a setting that's hard to beat. On an outside terrace in the courtyard of the villa, surrounded by geraniums, greenery and ancient flaking walls, tables are spread under umbrellas. A range of pizzas, including

Risotto all'amarone

This traditional Veronese recipe uses amarone, but if you don't want to spend a fortune, or you want to keep the amarone for drinking, you could also try it with another rich red wine. Riso Nano Vialone Veronese is Verona's best risotto rice.

olive oil
crushed garlic
1 finely chopped onion
400 g Riso Nano Vialone Veronese
500 ml amarone
500 ml vegetable stock
75 g parmesan
salt and pepper to taste

1. Heat the oil in a large saucepan and add the garlic and onion. Cook the onion gently until transparent.
2. In another pan heat the stock.
3. Add the rice to the oil, garlic and onion and stir until coated.
4. Gradually add half the wine, stirring well and allowing the wine to be absorbed before adding any more liquid.
5. Simmer the stock and add the remaining wine.
6. Add the stock and wine mixture to the rice a little at a time, allowing it to be absorbed before adding any more. Keep stirring.
7. When the stock has been absorbed, remove the saucepan from the heat and stir in the parmesan, salt and pepper to taste. Allow to rest for a minute then stir and serve.

some with real buffalo mozzarella, there are also some good fish dishes and you can round the meal off with a delicious pink grapefruit sorbet.

Gelaterias

Gelateria, via Ingelheim 28. *Tue-Sun 1500-2130.* Despite the modesty of not giving itself a name other than Gelateria, this place is worth the trip out of town all on its own. The pistacchio actually looks and tastes like pistacchio nuts, the chocolate is rich and dark and the fruit flavours have plenty of fruit in them.

Soave and the southern plains

Restaurants

€€€ Enacoteca il Drago, piazza dell'Antenna, **T/F** 045 7680670. *Tue-Sun 0900-1500, 1800-0130.* In the centre of Soave, in a medieval deconsecrated church, this excellent restaurant has tables under the arches with views down via Roma. Food is smart and traditional, with delicious pasta dishes. There is also the option of wine tasting: six different glasses of Soave for €7.75.

€€ Casablanca Café, via Roma 27, **T** 045 7680673. *Thu-Tue 0800-1500, 1800-0200.* A very stylish, but rather overdone, wine bar and restaurant, Casablanca has art deco lamps, fan, phone and screen. It also has piles of magazines, jazz, cigars, and cutlery which comes tied with a yellow ribbon. The wine list is as excellent as you'd expect, service is helpful but laid-back and the panini, which come served on wooden boards, are delicious. There are also a couple of fish options. In non-Casablanca style, it is also air-conditioned.

Valeggio sul Mincio

Restaurants

€€ **Ristorante Al Cacciatore**, via Goito 31, **T** 045 7950500,
F 045 6370375, www.alcacciatore.net *Closed Wed evening and all
day Thu.* Larger than many of Valeggio's restaurants, and also
slightly smarter, Al Cacciatore loses out in the homely stakes, but not
in its cuisine, which is still handmade, and exemplary. The tortellini
are excellent. Other specialities include trout with grilled polenta and
beef fillet cooked in amarone wine. Al Cacciatore also has rooms if
you should eat too much to be able to move far afterwards.

€ **Trattoria La Lanterna**, via Circonvallazione Sud,
T 045 7952087, la.lanterna@virgilio.it *Mon-Tue, Fri-Sun 1200-1400,
1930-2130.* With the archetypal Valeggio homely atmosphere,
Trattoria La Lanterna has tables outside on what still looks a little like
a drive, and a room inside where you don't feel too far removed from
a Veneto family Sunday lunch. The famous tortellini are light and
tasty and generously soaked in butter. Second courses are also very
good, with fish and meat options. Dishes change with the seasons,
but may include fresh octopus salad and succulent steak.

Cafés

La Fiaba, via M Buonarroti 38, Borghetto, **T** 045 7950055. *Tue
2100-0200, Wed-Sun 1800-0200.* This laid-back café has copious
quantities of candles, a verdant garden and 72 types of tea and 20
more infusions. At €4.20 though, they are overpriced. Cocktail and
other drinks are better value. The atmosphere swings slowly
between quiet and soporific.

Vicenza

Restaurants

€€ **Ristorante Pizzeria Paradiso**, via Pescherie Vecchie 5,
T 0444 322320. *Tue-Sun 1200-1430, 1900-0000. Map 3, E5, p254*
Excellent, juicy pizzas as well as a good range of standard fare
including pasta, meat and fish dishes mean the outside area fills up
with locals fairly quickly, and the atmosphere is lively.

€ **Righetti**, piazza Duomo 3, **T** 0444 543135. *Mon-Fri 1200-1430,
1900-2230. Map 3, F3, p254* This self-styled 'gourmet self-service'
restaurant is really a high quality canteen, with a good range of
standards such as baccalà and pasta all for good-value prices. A
warren of rooms means it isn't ever too hard to find a table.

Cafés

Caffè Natura, via Cesare Battista 17, **T** 0444 235372.
Map 3, E3, p254 All white marble and white-painted wood, this
café has a great selection of freshly squeezed juices, milkshakes
and yoghurt drinks as well as coffee and sandwiches.

Mantova

Restaurants

€€€€ **Leoncino Rosso**, via Giustiziati 33, **T** 0376 323277. *Tue-Sat
1130-1500, 1830-2400, closed for 2 weeks in Aug. Map 4, E6, p255* A
combination of *trattoria*, bar and *panificio* (bakers), Leoncino
Rosso, just off piazza Broletto, is a good place for food, some of
Mantova's excellent bread and cakes, or just a drink. Open since

Café society
Shops, cafés and a cinema line the porticoes of a Vicenza Street.

The line between Italian bars and restaurants is a fine one. *Osterie* serve food of varying complexity and *trattorie* often have good, and enormously long, wine lists. There is little tradition of drinking without eating, so the difference is generally one of emphasis – the places in this chapter place drinking above food in importance. In many, however, you can also get an excellent selection of snacks, or even a perfectly good meal. Having said that, Verona's student population add a lively edge to many of the city's drinking spots and some stay open well into the early hours. Wine predominates, though most places also have beer on tap and more interesting and adventurous places such as Al Mascaron and Square mix cocktails, too. Having an aperitivo before eating is traditional and pavement tables can get busy in the early evening, though less so than in some other Italian cities. Most cafés (see Eating and drinking, p133) also serve alcohol. Verona is poorly served by clubs, most of the area's big discos being scattered around the lower shores of Lake Garda.

Centro storico

Bars

Bottega del Vino, vicolo Scudo di Francia 3, **T** 045 8004535. *Mon, Wed-Sun 1030-1500, 1800-0000. Map 2, H5, p252* One of the city's oldest and most traditional bars, on a small street off via Mazzini, Bottega del Vino retains its medieval feel, with frescoed walls, wooden tables, chairs and benches, and 120 wines to choose from. The menu is also steadfast in its traditional Veronese format, with polenta, *lardo, risotto all'Amarone* and horse *pastisada*. Prices, however, have left those of ancient times far behind and skyrocketed, to make it one of Verona's most expensive bars.

Caffè Malta, piazzetta Navona 8, **T** 045 8030530. *Mon-Sat 0730-0200. Map 2, G6, p252* Open all day as a café, Malta comes into its own in the evenings when the atmosphere cranks up a notch or two, as does the volume. Despite the strange suit-and-tie art, the interior is an attractive mix of old walls, exposed pipes and wooden beams. Cocktails are made with panache but there is also beer on tap and the atmosphere is friendly. There's also a good seating area outside in the piazza – not Verona's most beautiful, but less touristy than most.

Camelot, via Leoncino 7, **T** 045 8001096. *Tue-Sun 1700-0200. Map 2, I7, p252* For a slightly bizarre Italian pub experience it's hard to beat the dim and cavernous Camelot, where a distinctly Italian view of British-/Irish-ness mixes with some very Italian habits. There is Guinness, Bombardier and Kilkenny on tap, grammatically incorrect English graffiti, a Scottish flag and a Union Jack, coffee and bar snacks, Gothic seats and candles, rock music and lots of Italians drinking halves.

Cappa Café, piazzetta Bra Molinari 1, **T** 045 8004516. *Daily 0800-0200*. *Map 2, D7, p252* This café/restaurant/bar is open late with plenty of choice of where to sit – either in the square outside, inside in one of the atmospheric rooms, or on the small terrace beside the river. Live music every Sunday. See also p141 and p166.

Carro Armato, vicolo Gatto 2a, **T** 045 8030175. *Mon and Tue, Thu-Sat 1100-0200, Sun 1100-0000*. *Map 2, E7, p252* One of Verona's most attractive bars, the large Carro Armato buzzes in the evenings, when it's usually full with a fairly young crowd sitting on its wooden benches against a backdrop of carefully cultivated flaking walls. The wine list is excellent, as is the simple but delicious food (see also p140). Friendly, accessible and one of the city's best places for late night socializing.

Highlander, via Leoncino 11, **T** 045 8002261. *1130-1500, 1800-0200, closed Wed*. *Map 2, I6, p252* Highlander, supposedly furnished entirely with authentic Scottish pub furniture, was for a long time the location of choice for many of Verona's students and trendy young. It's beginning to look a little tired these days, and has been eclipsed somewhat by Camelot just down the road, but there is still Old Speckled Hen and Newcastle Brown Ale on tap.

M27 Caffè, via Mazzini 27/a, **T** 045 8034242, *Tue-Sun 0830-0200*. *Map 2, H6, p252* An unusually young, modern and jazzy café and cocktail bar set back from via Mazzini whose drinks include non-alcoholic yoghurt cocktails and frozen margaritas. There is also a limited menu of crostini, salads and sandwiches. Internet use is available, most of the time, and the place comes into its own on weekend nights when it fills up with Verona's young, hip and upwardly mobile.

Osteria Sottoriva, via Sottoriva 9a, **T** 045 8014323. *Mon-Fri 1030-2230*. *Map 2, E7, p252* The most traditional of via Sottoriva's excellent selection of eating and drinking possibilities, this small *osteria* has battered old wooden tables under the arches which fill up quickly, mainly with ageing locals at lunchtime, and with young people in the evenings. More a drinking place than an eatery, the food is simple but nevertheless good, with horse, vegetables, pasta and excellent meatballs being the mainstays. The wine-list has improved under the new ownership of the Marquis of Fumanelli, who took over in early 2003. Make it an early stop rather than a late one, however, as it closes inhospitably early.

Osteria Verona, piazza Erbe 34, **T** 045 8030888. *Mon, Wed-Sun 1030-0200. Map 2, F5, p252* A corner of piazza Erbe reclaimed from the touristy cafés by the beautiful people of Verona. Especially at weekends the drinkers spill out of this little bar far into the piazza late into the night, with beer as much as wine the tipple of choice.

Sottoriva 23, 23 via Sottoriva, **T** 045 8009904. *Mon-Sun 1030-0230. Map 2, E7, p252* With tables outside on one of the city's most atmospheric streets, Sottoriva 23 soon fills up with Verona's young and trendy. There is an excellent menu of about 30 whiskies, a similar number of bottled beers, plus cocktails, wine and simple food. Monday evenings sees *Lounge Atmosphere*, with chill out and music from 1970s erotic movies, Tuesday is *Degustazione*, with wine, poetry and food, on Thursdays there is live acoustic music and on Sundays *Happyritivo* includes a free buffet, usually of pasta dishes.

Square, via Sottoriva 13-15, **T/F** 045 597120, www.squaresite.net *Tue-Fri 1830-0200, Sat and Sun 1530-0200. Map 2, E7, p252* Verona's grooviest nightspot is a furniture shop-cum-cocktail bar. Downstairs, a barista with attitude mixes drinks, while in a converted barrel-vaulted cellar, young *Veronesi* lounge on basket cube chairs in a strikingly modern and vaguely oriental setting, behind white floor-to-ceiling thread curtains. DJ sets of chilled soul with a slight edge play while light glows behind bamboo patterned panels. None of this super hipness gives any sense of coldness, however: there is no dress code, written or unwritten, and the place has a welcoming, friendly and laid-back vibe. Upstairs, at a capuccino bar, there is free internet use, very cool minimalist furniture to buy, a CD-listening area with more avant garde new tunes, and a shop area selling expensive retro sunglasses, studio ceramics and design books. Not to be missed.

Taverna Degli Scaligeri, via Sottoriva 24, **T** 045 590302. *Tue-Sun 1900-0200. Map 2, E7, p252* An Italian-style tavern, Degli Scaligeri has no fake Irish theming, but beer is still the main drink of choice, with Hoegarden, Leffe and Franziskaner among the beers on tap. Wine is also available, and there's a limited menu, too. There are attractive wooden benches, but the always-on TV is a little off-putting.

Clubs

Caffè Bukowski, via Amanti 6, no **T**. *Mon, Wed-Sun 1900-0200. Map 2, H7, p252* Though it calls itself a café, and is open early in the evening as a bar, with beers on tap, nobody much seems to turn up until at least 2200, and the atmosphere is certainly one of a club. White drapes, a black ceiling, mirror balls, ultraviolet lights, cocktails, pink sequins, DJ sets and plenty of camp attitude.

South of the centro storico

Bars

Al Mascaron, piazza San Zeno 16, **T** 045 597081. *Mon, Wed-Sun, 0830-1430, 1730-2330, Tue 1730-0130. Map 1, D1, p250* Venue of the moment for Verona's young and trendy, the crowds spill out from this colourful cocktail bar far into San Zeno's piazza. The bar, if you can get near it, is decorated with a variety of low-level lights, tiles, fish, and an underwater marine colour scheme. During the day it's much quieter, but equally full of attitude.

Enoteca Cangrande, via Dietro Listone 19d, **T** 045 595022, enoteca.cangrande@zyme.it *Mon-Sat 1100-1400, 1700-0100. Map 2, J3, p252* A wine shop as well as an atmospheric wine bar, Cangrande, just behind piazza Bra, attracts a smart brand of locals at lunchtime as well as in the evening when food such as polenta with mushrooms and cheese is also available. There is a big selection of wine by the glass.

Clubs

Associazione Culturale Interzona, 16 via Santa Teresa, **T** 045 505005. www.izona.it *Map 1, J4, p250* Interzona, a left-leaning social group, have their base in an old refrigeration warehouse. Though it's not a club in the standard sense of the word, there are occasional nights there of excellent, often avant garde, music, both DJs and live concerts, and an excellent youthful atmosphere. The place is also used for exhibitions. It's not at all easy to get to though, in the heart of Verona's industrial southern sector. If you don't have your own transport a taxi is recommended.

North and east of the Adige

Bars

Ai Preti, via Interrato dell'Acqua Morta 27, **T** 045 597675. *Mon-Sat 1900-0200. Map 2, H8, p252* A healthy mix of tattoos, students and university professors during the evenings and ageing regulars during the day, Preti is a good left-field wine bar with an excellent atmophere, good wine drunk in generous quantities, reasonable prices and no pretensions to grandeur. The name is said to come from a time when priests were given their own special entrance to allow them to frequent the place anonymously.

Clubs

Alter Ego, via Torricelle 9, **T** 045 915130. *Summer only. Fri and Sat 2100-0400, plus occasional other nights. Check www.alteregoclub.it or press for details.* Far enough out of town for the disco beats not to carry back, Alter Ego, in the hills above the city, has a terrace outside, looking back over Verona. It's a colourful, trendy place, with vaguely alternative sounds, and mainly Italian DJs, but it's not easy to get to without your own transport.

Berfi's, via Lussemburgo 1, **T** 045 508024, www.berfis.com *Fri-Sun 2300-0400. Map 1, 1M, p250* In the industrial south of the city, Berfi's is popular but fairly conventional, with lots of pop hits. There is a *Caffè degli Artisti* area with live music and cabaret, and from 2030 until 2330 the entrance price includes a meal at the attached Il Cantuccio restaurant. In summer Berfi's moves to the Lido at Torri del Benaco on Lake Garda (see p84).

Lago di Garda

Clubs

Hollywood Danceclub, via Montefelice 11, Bardolino, **T** 045 7210580, www.hollywood.it *Thu-Sun 2200-0400.* On the hill of Bardolino, with a great view of the lake, Hollywood Danceclub is possibly the trendiest of Garda's clubs. With a main room, a private room and a garden, and a mix of colonial and mediterranean styles, Thursday to Sunday evenings have international guests and events as well as happy house and '70s and '80s tunes.

Arts and entertainment

Whereas most other Italian cities go to sleep in the summer as the population heads for the cooler hills and coasts, Verona comes alive, transforming from a relatively lethargic place into a vibrant mix of musical and cultural enthusiasm. At the heart of this is the city's famous opera season in July and August, but world-class jazz, pop music and theatre in particular have grabbed onto the coat-tails of the city's annual cultural celebration. Few cities can boast two such spectacular performance spaces as the Arena and the Teatro Romano, and excellent international stars seem only too happy to come and use them. Outside of the summer season Verona has other cultural attractions, primary among which is the traditional Teatro Filarmonico, but also the avant-garde Interzona, an adapted ex-freezer-warehouse in the industrial south of the city. *Veronalive* (www.veronalive.it) is a bi-monthly listings magazine with up-to-the-minute information on what's going on around the city.

Cinema

Of Verona's cinemas, only one ever has original language foreign films, and then not very regularly. Neither is there much of an arts cinema scene, the city's central cinemas all serving a fairly bland diet of mainstream films. Even Verona's film heritage is strictly limited to not much more than Zeffirelli's 1968 rendition of Romeo and Juliet. Two small film festivals lift the standards slightly: Festival del cinema Africano in February and March, and Schermi d'Amore in April (see Festivals, p184).

Astra, via Oberdan, **T** 045 596327. *Map 2, I3, p252* One of central Verona's few memorable 20th-century buildings, the Astra shows fairly standard fare.

Filarmonico, via Roma 2, **T** 045 596826. *Map 2, J2, p252* More Hollywood dubbed into Italian near piazza Bra.

Teatro Stimate, via Montanari 1, **T** 045 8000878. *Map 2, L4, p252* Films in lingua originale every Tuesday evening from September to June.

Dance

The Teatro Romano (see Theatre, below) has a limited summer dance season in July and August, with some interesting modern touring groups visiting. Recent events have included Viennese opera and the Compaña Tango por Dos. Otherwise productions are limited to occasional touring visits, and occasional city council organized productions in the central piazzas.

Music

Once the summer season of Arena and Teatro Romano spectaculars dies away, the Teatro Filarmonico takes over as the primary space for music, especially classical, though there is also a jazz season here (see Festivals, p185). Other venues around the city also host classical recitals, such as those organized by the city council in the central piazzas, or in the courtyard of Juliet's house. Again, however, these are usually confined to the summer months, but are mostly free. The church of San Bernardino (see p67) also holds occasional classical concerts, as does Castelvecchio (see p57).

Big international pop acts also use the Arena for concerts, which hosted Björk and Massive Attack in 2003. Less likely venues for international superstars include the pool and spa complex at Caldiero (see p97) which James Brown graced with his presence in 2003. Cutting edge sounds can be heard on a rather irregular basis at Interzona, otherwise local live music tends to be of a more laid-back variety. Bars and cafés with regular live music include Cappa Café (Sunday afternoons, see p141 and p166) and Invidia (via San Vitale,19/a, **T** 045 596926. *Mon-Fri 0800-1900, 2100-0400, Sat 1900-0400*. Live music every Friday and Saturday from October to March. Veronese groups predominate).

Both the Teatro Romano (summer) and the Teatro Filarmonico (spring) have excellent jazz seasons, with big international names being attracted especially to the former.

Classical

Teatro Filarmonico, via dei Mutilati 4, **T** 045 8051891, **F** 045 8031443, www.arena.it   *Tickets, via Roma 3, 1000-1200, 1630-1930, or until 2100 on performance days. Booking line* **T** *045 8005151,* **F** *045 8013287.*   *Map 2, J3, p252*   The building, rebuilt after the Second World War, has never quite recovered the prestige it had in its glory days at the beginning of the 18th century. Its first incarnation, designed by Bibiena in 1716, was almost completely destroyed by fire in 1749. The latest version remains impressively grand inside and is still a fine concert space attracting some very good international names. Concerts are usually traditional, but are well-attended by well-dressed locals.

Scuola Civica Musicale, via Lega Veronese 10/a, **T/F** 045 8030325 (*enquiries 1500-1830*). *Map 1, C1, p250* The Civic School of Music organizes occasional evening concerts. Mostly classical, but occasionally also jazz.

Eclectic and modern

Interzona, Stazione Frigorifera Specializzata 10, ex Magazini Generali, via Santa Teresa 16, **T** 045 505005. www.izona.it *Map 1, J4, p250* At the heart of just about everything cutting edge that happens in the city, Interzona organizes exhibitions, installations, film and music events in a giant disused ex-refrigeration plant in the industrial heartland in the south of the city. Buses being very infrequent around the southern parts of the city, you may have to get a taxi, or be prepared to walk a long way through a less salubrious area of town.

Jazz

A summer season in the Teatro Romano (see p71 and p180) and a winter sesason in the Teatro Filarmonico (see p174) both attract big names, some of whom even graduate to the Arena for popular concerts. Outside of these, however, there is little regular jazz around, though it's always worth checking local listings for special events.

★ **Post-opera restaurants**

- Trattoria Tre Marchetti, p143.
- Tre Corone, p144.
- Le Cantine de L'Arena, p144.
- Osteria Le Vecete, p139.
- Trattoria a Lanterna, p146.

Opera

Arena, piazza Bra, booking line **T** 045 8005151, **F** 045 8013287, www.arena.it Box office, 6/b via Dietro Anfiteatro, 37121 Verona (*Mon-Fri 0900-1200, 1515-1745, Sat 0900-1200, 21 Jun-1 Aug performance days 1000-2100, non-performance days 1000-1745*). *Map 2, I/J4, p253* The world's most spectacular opera theatre was rediscovered as a performance space in 1913, when Aida was first performed there. The summer opera season is now a firm event on the European calendar. Enormous, epic, traditional productions of the best known operas are the Arena's stock in trade, and Verona's most successful tourist attraction. Franco Zeffirelli directed the lavish 2003 productions of Carmen, Aida, Rigoletto, Nabucco and Turandot. Operas are alternated every night so that even those staying for a long weekend can see two or three operas if they want.

Tickets can be bought over the phone, via the website, in person from the box office or a number of other outlets or by post, enclosing a bank draft and specifying the date of the performance, the seat sector and the number of tickets required. Tickets range in price from € 17.50 (€ 14 for under 26s and the over 60s) for a seat on the Roman steps high above the stage, to € 154 for a central seat near the action. In order to book online it is necessary to first register, though the process is fairly straightforward and there are instructions in English.

Up until mid-June tickets are posted out. After this they must be collected from the box office in person.

During performances various people squeeze down the rows renting cushions (€2.50, highly recommended in the cheap seats), and selling drinks and ice-creams, rather ineffective binoculars, programmes and librettos. Candles aren't obligatory, but are traditional and add to the atmosphere, everyone lighting up just before the show begins. Librettos are also widely (and cheaply) available in English from local bookshops if you want to check up on the storyline beforehand. There is no dress code, but the more expensive seats tend to fill up with the most expensive suits and dresses. Performances start around 2100 and generally last three or four hours. To have a choice of seats in the unreserved higher tiers it may be necessary to turn up an hour and a half or so before. Bear in mind that on hot days the stone steps of the Arena get very hot and continue to radiate unwelcome heat long into the night. On such occasions seats on the east side (starting in sector 'A') are better than those opposite, where the sun leaves last, and where spectators can often be seen frantically waving fans. Most bars and restaurants around the Arena itself, especially those in piazza Bra, stay open late to catch the post-opera appetites, though given the sudden influx of people, booking ahead is advisable if you want a table. See box ("Best 5 post-opera eats"), p176. Many restaurants also open earlier than usual on opera days to cater for pre-opera eating.

Theatre

Verona's best theatre, and the only real international theatre, happens in the Estate Teatrale Veronese season at the Teatro Romano. There are a few other theatres scattered around the city, but they generally show fairly turgid fare.

▶ A beginner's guide to opera

Opera as a form of exaggerated musical drama was invented in the latter part of the 16th century around Florence, in Tuscany, 190 km to the south of Verona. Initially a Renaissance attempt to recapture the tragic dramas of ancient Greece, it became one of music's most predominant forms.

The first work to be called an opera was *Dafne*, composed by Jacopo Peri and written by poet Ottavio Rinuccini for the wedding of Henry IV of France to Maria de Medici in 1600. Monteverdi (1567-16430) developed the genre with an emotional expressiveness which is now one of its most famous characteristics.

Mozart composed operas such as *The Marriage of Figaro* and *The Magic Flute* in the 18th century, further enhancing the dramatic nature of the form. It wasn't until the 19th century, however, that opera reached its peak, with composers such as Verdi, Bizet, Rossini, Wagner, Puccini and even Beethoven producing ever more lavish and grandiose productions.

At the turn of the 20th century Opera gave birth to operetta (literally, little opera), a genre which contains some speech, and then, in America, to musicals. Opera, however, differs from its descendents in that the music and singing is continuous – there is no spoken dialogue, only the sung words of the libretto, or text.

Opera traditionally begins with an overture, a musical introduction to the themes and musical highlights of the action to come. There then follow arias, songs sung just by a soloist, and ensembles, which are duets, trios, quartets and so on. As well as the soloists there is a chorus, who both sing the backing to the soloists and can have songs of their own. There can also be supers, non-singing actors. Meanwhile, a full orchestra provides the musical backdrop, while the conductor waves his baton and holds the whole thing together.

Glossary

aria - From the Italian for 'air', a song for a solo voice with instrumental accompaniment. Like a theatrical monologue, it often takes the audience into the thoughts and feelings of the character.

baritone - The mid-toned male singing voice, between the low bass and the higher tenor.

bass - The lowest male voice.

bel canto - From the Italian for 'beautiful song'. In bel canto style, the beauty of singing is the most important aspect.

bravo!/brava!/bravi! - Literally, 'well done', expressed to a man/a woman/more than one person. The traditional operatic shout of appreciation.

cadenza - A series of high fast notes at the end of an aria, used to demonstrate vocal virtuosity.

castrato - A castrated male whose unbroken voice stays high all his life.

crescendo - A progressive increase in volume.

diminuendo - A progressive decrease in volume.

diva - From the Italian for 'goddess', a female opera star. Has connotations of self-importance, as does prima donna, or first lady.

entr'acte - a musical piece between acts or scenes.

finale - the last song of an act, usually a grand piece with lots of singers. The *finale ultimo* is the last finale of the opera.

imbroglio - From the Italian for 'confusion', a scene in which different rhythms and tunes create deliberate chaos.

leitmotiv - a short piece of music representing a character or other element of the drama.

libretto - Literally, 'little book'. The text of an opera, written by the librettist. Available in bookshops all over Verona, usually with English translations and plot synopses.

maestro - A term of respect for the conductor.

soprano - The highest voice, usually female.

tenor - The highest male voice, between baritone and alto.

trouser role - a male character sung by a woman.

Teatro Romano, Regaste Redentore 2, **T** 045 8000360, www.estateteatraleveronese.it *Tickets, Palazzo Barbieri, via degli Alpini 2, **T** 045 8066485/**T** 045 8066488, Mon-Sat, also Sun if performance day, 1030-1300, 1600-1900. Map 2, C8, p252 See also p71* Since 1948, when Romeo and Juliet was first performed here, Shakespeare has become an annual fixture. A high quality British production is usually the centrepiece of the burgeoning Estate Teatrale Veronese (see also Festivals and events, p185), the Verona summer theatre festival, which now encompasses a wide range of entertainment.

By far the city's biggest event, the summer opera season dominates other events and many hang off its coat-tails, concentrating cultural events in the city in July and August. Some of these other summer events have become very successful in their own rights, however, such as the jazz and theatre festivals. The city's second big people puller is *Vinitaly*, when everything and everyone wine-related pours into Verona. Other fairs which tend to fill the city's hotels are the horse and marble events. Outside of these peaks of activity there are plenty of other traditions and special seasons, however, such as the pre-Christmas Santa Lucia, Carnevale or music at the Teatro Filarmonico. A bit further afield Mantova has an excellent literature festival, and Torbole has international windsurfing competitions. Then there is the Verona marathon, and the less competitive StraVerona, or the completely uncompetitive *Magnalonga*, a wine-drinking, food-eating, mass-participation walking tour of Valpolicella.

January

Capodanno (1st) New Year. Look out for news of special events at places such as Interzona (see p169).

February

Carnevale (February or March) A procession follows a traditionally small, fat character, *Papà del Gnoco*, through the streets of Verona, culminating with a *gran gnocolada* in piazza San Zeno, where free gnocchi are distributed. Annual elections for the post of Papà are said to be more important than those for politicians.

Festival del Cinema Africano (February and March) With collaboration from the university and the diocesan missionary, Verona's African film festival first took place in 1981 and was the first in Italy. Films are shown at the Cinema Kappadue (via Rosmini 1/b, T 045 8005895)

March

Pasqua (Easter) Various celebrations and events mark the Easter weekend. There is a Good Friday procession and on the Saturday there is a regatta on the Adige. On Easter Monday there is the traditional eating of *pasta fagioli* (pasta with beans). Easter Sunday is reserved for religious solemnity.

Vinitaly (End of March to mid-April) Italy's most important wine fair takes place at the Fiera, to the south of the old city (see p70), with producers, buyers and consumers from all over the world. In 2002 there were 3,858 exhibitors from 24 foreign countries and 161,721 visitors. www.vinitalyonline.com

Festa dei Vini Classici della Valpolicella (late April- early May) The highlight of two weeks of Valpolicella-related activities is *Magnalonga*, a Sunday where over 2,000 people take part in a sort of vineyard-crawl starting in Pedemonte and visiting local *cantine*. At each stop participants are rewarded with a glass of local wine, food, and local bands destroying various American rock/blues classics. The atmosphere starts off genial enough and becomes even more so with each stop. € 18. **T/F** 045 6850159, www.magnalonga.com

Schermi d'Amore. Festival of romance films based in the Cinema Filarmonico (see p173). The focus is mostly mainstream and sentimental but there are also some more interesting films.

May

Le Piazze dei Sapori (a long weekend in mid-May) Stalls in the piazzas to the southeast of piazza dei Signori (from cortile Mercato Vecchio to piazzetta Pescheria) bring local and national produce to the city centre, with plenty of free tasters to tempt you to buy. Live music in piazza dei Signori accompanies the event in the evenings. www.lepiazzedeisapori.com

StraVerona (a Sunday in mid-May) Over 10,000 people run or walk three routes of varying length and seriousness (5, 12 and 21 km) in and around the city. A € 5 ticket, available the day before in piazza Bra, gets you a pack of local goodies including wine and olive oil, as well as refreshments en route, and free entrance to the Arena and the city's museums for the whole weekend. Associazione StraVerona, viale Sicilia 11, **T** 045 562653.

June

Arena di Verona (mid-June to the end of August) The 82nd festival of opera in Verona's Roman amphitheatre in 2004 will include Aida (as ever) and Madame Butterfly among its offerings. Information, Fondazione Arena di Verona, piazza Bra 28. Tickets via Dietro Anfiteatro 6/b (opposite the Arena 'wing'), **T** 045 8005151, **F** 045 8013287, www.arena.it See also p54.

Estate Teatrale Veronese (End of June to beginning of September) Based around the tradition of Shakespeare in the Teatro Romano, Verona's summer theatre festival usually includes performances of a high-quality English language Shakespeare by the likes of the RSC or the Watermill Theatre. It has also widened its remit to include dance, however, and in 2003 both tango and Viennese ballet graced the Roman stage. Some interesting smaller productions are also held in the cortile Mercato Vecchio, and even in the courtyard of the Casa di Giulietta. Information, **T** 045 8077201. www.estateteatraleveronese.it Tickets, Palazzo Barbieri, via degli Alpini 2, **T** 045 8066485 *(Mon-Sat and Sun on days with performances1030-1300, 1600-1900)*.

Verona Jazz (End of June to mid-July) For around three weeks in the middle of summer Verona overflows with jazz talent. An off-shoot of the theatre festival, concerts are held almost every night, mostly in the excellent setting of the Teatro Romano, but also in the cortile Mercato Vecchio, piazza dei Signori, and even in the Arena. Recent performers have included the Jan Garbarek Group, the Ron Carter Quartet, the Diana Krall Quartet and less well known artists from Macedonia and Cuba. Performances in piazzas are sometimes free. Tickets start at €6. Information, **T** 045 8077201. www.estateteatraleveronese.it Tickets, Palazzo

Barbieri, via degli Alpini 2, **T** 045 8066485 *(Mon-Sat and Sun on days with performances1030-1300, 1600-1900).*

July

Opera in Concerto (End of July to beginning of August) As if Verona was not already saturated with all things operatic in high summer, this new festival brings arias and overtures from opera to the cloister of San Luca, just to the south of piazza Bra, in concert form. Advance tickets from Box Office Verona, via Pallone 12/a, **T** 045 8011154. On the day of the concert, Chiostro di San Luca, corso Porta Nuova 12, *0930-1200, 1700-2100.* info@operainconcerto.it

Garda Trentino Formula Windsurfing Youth World Championship One of the major events traditionally held off the windy shores of Torbole on Lake Garda is the Youth Windsurfing World Championship.

August

Ferragosto (Feast of the Assumption, Aug 15th) celebrated with water fights, water melon and a frenzied light-hearted air of summer holiday. Most Italians leave the city for the sea, the mountains or the lake.

September

Festivaletteratura (beginning of month) For five or six days in Mantova, Italian and international authors gather for a big literature festival. Events take place in the city's piazzas, cloisters, and palazzos. In 2003 participants included Alain de Botton, Peter Carey, Simon Armitage, Ian McEwan and Irvine Welsh. **T** 0376 223989, **F** 0376 367047, www.festivaletteratura.it

Festival di Musica Antica (September to November but also in May) In Vicenza, a festival so spread out it hardly warrants the name, has baroque music in the churches, courtyards and palazzos of the city, and even in the Teatro Olimpico. Some concerts are free. www.spaziomusica.it Information and tickets from tourist information in Vicenza, **T** 0444 320854, **F** 0444 327072.

Marmomacc (September or October) An international stone, marble and building fair, considered one of the city's most important, takes place at the Fiera. www.marmomacc.com

---

October

Maratona di Verona (Sunday) Alongside the traditional 26-and-a-bit mile race, there is also a disabled marathon, a rollerblade marathon, a vintage car marathon and a marathon of prayer. **T** 045 8183847, www.maratonadiverona.it

Jazz al Filarmonico (October to May) Throughout the winter, an elongated season of jazz at the Teatro Filarmonico, interspersed with the more traditional classical season, attracts some good international names.

November

Fiera Cavalli One of the city's oldest fairs, the horse fair, takes place at the Fiera.

December

Rassegna del Presepio (all month) In the arches of the Arena an international exhibition of nativity scenes takes place.

Though smaller, family-run shops are relatively rare by Italian standards, and good markets even more so, the city does well for Italian high-street shopping. Smart clothes and shoe shops line via Mazzini and corso Porta Borsari and there are some excellent kitchen shops, too, radiant with all the latest Italian shiny gadgetry for making coffee or pasta or slicing salami. There are a couple of fascinating antique/junk shops and a fantastic toy shop. There are plenty of wine shops, some of which offer enormous selections and stunning, atmospheric interiors, but they struggle to compete with the supermarkets on price. Supermarkets and delicatessens also offer excellent Italian food, some of which, such as parmesan, is easier to transport home than others. For Italian design, other than the slick kitchen shops, there are homeware and furnishing shops where you can often buy the simplest items for enormous pricetags, but also beautiful rugs and lights.

Antiques

Cavaliere, stradone Porta Palio 41, **T** 329 8977848. *Mon-Sat 0930-1300, 1700-1900. Map 1, F3, p250* A mix of antique furniture, second-hand leather briefcases, vases, hat boxes and other period bits and pieces. Quality is much more reliable than in Mercatino dell'Usato just down the road, but prices are also much higher.

Mercatino dell'Usato, stradone Porta Palio 33, **T** 340 0061499. *Mon-Sat 1100-1300, 1600-2000. Map 1, E3, p250* A mix of junk and antiques. Rubber spiders, antique furniture, euro calculators, pewter jugs, dusty wine glasses, videos, books, comics and all sorts of other hidden treasures are piled high waiting to be uncovered.

Art

My Collection, via Sottoriva 12, **T/F** 045 8013966, my.collection@tiscali.net *Tue-Sat 1000-1300, 1600-2000. Map 2, F7, p252* Verona's best private gallery has an interesting and sometimes humorous collection of modern paintings and photos, as well as good temporary exhibitions.

Tipografia Arche Scaligeri, via S Maria in Chiavica 3c, **T/F** 045 8003392, tipoarche@libero.it *Mon-Fri 0900-1230, 1530-1900. Map 2, F6, p252* A print workshop since 1750, Tipografia Arche Scaligeri has etchings of the city for sale starting at around € 45. They also print business cards and stationery.

Bookshops

Ghelfi & Barbato, via Mazzini 21, **T** 045 597732. *Mon-Sat 0900-1230, 1530-1900. Map 2, H5, p252* In a prime position for the strolling hordes of via Mazzini, Ghelfi & Barbato keeps surprisingly unsociable hours compared to other bookshops around the city, but has English-speaking staff and a good food and drink section upstairs.

FNAC, via Cappello 34, **T** 045 8063811. *Mon-Sat 0930-2000, Sun 1030-2000. Map 2, H7, p252* Selling just about everything (Computers, cameras, TVs, CDs etc) FNAC, a sort of multi-media department store, has a good book department downstairs and an excellent events programme, with authors and musicians. There is also a café, whose walls are used as a photography exhibition space, and four internet terminals.

Gulliver, 16/b via Stella, **T** 045 8007234, www.gullivertravelbooks.it *Mon 1530-1930, Tue-Sat 0930-1230, 1530-1930. Map 2, H6, p252* This travel bookshop has an excellent selection of travel guides on just about everywhere except Verona, including English language guides. There is also an impressive number of illustrated books and the city's best selection of maps, including an enormous number covering walks and bike trails through the mountains to the north of the city.

Libreria Gheduzzi, 7 corso Sant'Anastasia, **T** 045 8002234. *Map 2, F5, p252* Excellent bookshop, almost always open. Good art, design and photography sections and a sociable café (see p141).

The Bookshop, 3/a Interrato dell'Acqua Morta, **T/F** 045 8007614, bookshopvr@libero.it *Mon 1530-1930, Tue-Fri 0930-1230, 1530-1930. Map 2, H8, p252* An international bookshop, with plenty of books in English, The Bookshop caters mainly for students and so has a range weighted heavily in favour of classics, but also has some modern novels.

Clothes

Most high street Italian chains, such as Stefanel, Sisley, Diesel, MaxMara, Witboy and Pinkie, as well as more upmarket labels such as Gucci and Versace, have stores on via Mazzini. For more interesting clothes there are fewer options, though Mr Gulliver across the river has a good selection of sixties and seventies second-hand clothes alongside some new fashion.

Mr Gulliver, via S Vitale 7/e, **T** 045 8015642, **F** 045 8065944. *Map 1, D7, p250*

Department stores

UPIM, via Mazzini 6, **T** 045 596701. *Mon-Sat 0900-1930.* *Map 2, G6, p252* Four floors of Italian shopping, mainly rather plain clothes, but also BluCasa, a home and kitchen floor, and BluKids, with clothes for small people.

Coin, via Cappello 30, **T** 045 8034321. *Mon 1530-1930, Tue-Sat 0915-1230, 1530-1930. Map 2, F5, p252* Five floors of mostly women's fashion and cosmetics. Summer sales from mid-July to the end of August.

Food

De Rossi, 3 corso Porta Borsari, **T** 045 8002489. *Mon-Sat 0830-1930. Map 2, G4, p253* This mouth-watering shop describes itself as a *Panificio Pastificio Pasticceria Dietica*, which means it sells a great collection of freshly cooked bread, cakes and biscuits as well as pasta, jams, oils and health food. There is also a branch at via Albere 20/a.

Horses for courses
*Verona's delicatessens sell an excellent range of cheeses and meats,
including the ubiquitous Veronese favourite, horsemeat.*

Peter's Tea House, via dei Pellicciai 6, **T** 045 8034223,
verona@peters-teahouse.it *Map 2, G5, p252* Not exactly
traditional Veronese fare, but all the same, a good selection
of teas and tea paraphernalia, and a free cup of a speciality tea.

Caffè Tubino, 15/d corso Porta Borsari, **T** 045 8032296. *Daily
0700-2300. Map 2, G4, p252* Good for buying coffee as well as
drinking it (see p142).

La Salumeria, 33 corso Sant'Anastasia, **T** 045 592757. *Mon-Sat
0800-2000, Sun 0930-1300. Map 2, E6, p252* A small grocers,
crammed to the ceiling with high quality Italian produce: balsamic
vinegar, wine, olive oil, meat, cheese and penis-shaped pasta.

PAM, via dei Mulati 3, **T** 045 8032822. *Mon-Sat 0800-2000, Sun 0900-1330, 1500-1900. Map 2, K2, p252* The best supermarket in the centre of Verona, PAM has all you need for a great picnic, including a good fresh bread section and a delicatessen counter with a big selection of local cheeses and cold meats. It's also a good cheap place to buy wine and spirits to take home. Spirits offer the biggest savings compared to foreign prices, and are usually cheaper here than at "Duty Free" at the airport.

Home and lifestyle

Slamp, via Oberdan 11/c, **T** 045 8014204, www.slamp.it *Tue-Sat 1000-1230, 1600-1930. Map 2, H3, p252* Glassware, lights and dishes with a colourful twist, from the stylishly minimalist to the kitsch.

Kalin, via G Oberdan 12/b, **T** 045 8013422, giancarlo.zanessi@tin.it *Map 2, H4, p252* Beautiful but expensive rugs and carpets are available from this modern showroom near piazza Bra. Designs are both modern and ethnic.

il Ghibellin Fuggiasco, vicolo dietro SS Apostoli 7, **T** 045 8035557, **F** 045 8045448, www.ilghibellinfuggiasco.com *Sun and Mon 1530-1930, Tue-Sat 0930-1230, 1530-1930. Map 2, J1, p252* Beautiful designer bits and pieces for the kitchen and home. At over € 150 for a colander, however, likely to be beyond most people's budgets. Another branch at via XX Settembre 27 has equally extortionate furniture.

Kitchen

Fazzini, via Roma 21a. *Mon 1500-1930, Tue-Sat 0900-1230, 1500-1930. Map 2, J1, p252* Enormous selection of just about every type of shiny chrome gadgetry you could imagine, including an excellent selection of coffee-makers.

Leather

Wild Texas Cowboy, via S Paolo 11/a, **T** 340 3421272, www.wildtexas.it *Tue-Sun 0930-1230, 1530-1930. Map 2, I8, p252*
Wallets, stools, telescope cases and just about anything else are all handmade behind this small shop. As the name suggests, some articles have a wild west theme. Well-made handbags are a good alternative to the fake labels touted on via Mazzini.

Markets

Verona does poorly for markets, especially when compared to other Italian cities.

Mercato dello Stadio, piazzale Olimpia. *Saturday morning.* Market goods, including clothes and kitchen goods.

Mercato di piazza Erbe. A mix of fruit, vegetables and novelty lighters. Future still in doubt, see p105.

Mercato di Sottoriva, via Sottoriva, *2nd Saturday of the month.* Antiques.

Music

FNAC (see bookshops, above) has the best range in the centre of Verona, including an excellent *Nuovi Suoni* (New Sounds) section, and lots of listening posts.

Shoes

Corso Porta Borsari has plenty of smart shoe shops and lots of others are scattered around the centre. Good prices and quality.

Kammi, 17a via Leoni. *Mon 1530-1945, Tue-Sat 0900-1245, 1530-1945. Map 2, I7, p252* Stylish, but not absurdly expensive, women's shoes, generally made by smaller labels. Especially good sales in summer and winter.

Stationery

Lo Scrittoio, corso Porta Borsari 18, **T** 045 8035720. *Mon 1600-1945, Tue-Sat 0930-1245, 1600-1945. Map 2, G4, p252* A small shop selling upmarket writing equipment and stationery, with a great collection of desirable pens.

N R Saletti, via delle Fogge 6/a, **T** 045 8006849. *Mon-Fri 0900-1330, 1530-1930. Map 2, F5, p252* A small artists' supply shop near piazza dei Signori stacked high with paints, papers and pens.

Toys

Città del Sole, 8b via Cattaneo, **T** 045 591761. *Mon 1600-1930, Tue-Sat 0930-1230, 1600-1930. Map 2, I3, p252* One of Verona's most interesting shops, Città del Sole has things to attract just about everyone: globes, weathervanes, castles, hi-tech gadgets, bug-viewers, games, jigsaws, books, thermometers, bird feeders and, strangely, some new age background music.

Wine

If price is more important than atmosphere, choice and expertise, wine and other alcohol is often cheapest in supermarkets (see food, above).

Vintage Verona

Unaffected by the modern demands of tourism, this wine shop, on via Alberto Mario, just off piazza Bra, is the city's most atmospheric.

Vini Liquori, via A Mario 23, **T** 045 8002560. *Mon-Sat 1000-0030. Also some Sundays in summer. Map 2, I4, p252* A fantastic old wine shop with absolutely no trimmings, despite a prominent position just off piazza Bra. Tastings and cigarette smoke.

L'Enoteca, via Sottoriva 7/b, **T/F** 045 590366, www.enotecaverona.com *Tue-Sat 0930-1230, 1530-1930. Sun-Mon 1530-1930. Map 2, F7, p252* A smart place in the heart of the city's wine-drinking territory which takes itself and its wines seriously. Some 800 m of Roman and medieval cellars are suitably cool and dank. Long banqueting tables here make it a great place for the monthly wine-tasting events. Helpful, English-speaking staff.

Shopping

Sports

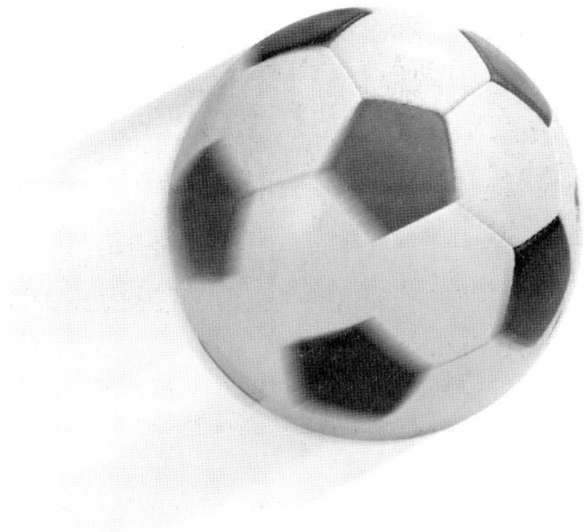

Hardly the most sporting place in the world, Verona has, nevertheless, two professional football teams, an annual marathon, and has ideal surroundings for watersports in summer and for skiing in winter. There are some good swimming pools, too, and since the Veronesi won't consider it swimming weather until it's well into the thirties, you can often have large expanses of sun-drenched pool all to yourself, especially outside of July and August. Lake Garda is the centre for watersports, in particular windsurfing, though some canoeing takes place on the river in the city centre. In a good winter, ski-lifts relatively close to the north of the city run for several months, otherwise it may be necessary to head for higher slopes. In the heat of summer it can be too hot for walking except on the higher mountains, but in spring and autumn the hills and mountains around have plenty of scope for walks and treks of just about any length, from afternoon strolls to month-long treks across the Alps.

Canoeing

Canoa Club Verona, via Filippini, **T** 349 6683448,
www.canoaclubverona.it € 180 for 5 lessons. *Map 2, J7, p252*
Verona's canoeing club offers lessons on the Adige, but isn't very
accommodating for visitors.

Cycling

There are some good cycling routes in the hills to the north of the
city. See p214 for details of cycle hire. On summer weekends APTV
run 'Bus & Bike' routes into Lessinia, transporting bikes and riders
up into the hills. **T** 045 8057911 or www.aptv.it for details. There is
a free map of cycle routes around Lake Garda available from tourist
information offices. Surf Segnana Windsurf (see windsurfing,
below) in Torbole also rent out mountain bikes.

Football

Verona's 42,160-capacity stadium, built in 1963, is home to two
teams, Hellas Verona, and Chievo, who now call themselves Chievo
Verona. Verona were Italian Serie 'A' champions in 1985, but have
struggled to stay in the top division ever since and are currently in
Serie 'B' after being dramatically relegated in 2002 on the last day
of the season. Chievo, the local upstarts, are from a suburb with a
population of only a few thousand. They became the feelgood
story of football the world over in 2001 when, for a time, their team
of anonymous no-hopers topped Serie 'A'. After two consecutive
top seven finishes and a European place for the 2002/2003 season,
they are now taken a lot more seriously, though their 'we are nice
local small-town people' attitude grates with many Hellas Verona
fans (see box, p202) as does the fact that they now play in Hellas's
stadium and in their colours. The stadium, an impressive but

The two teams of Verona

In October 2001, Chievo, the football team of a small Veronese suburb of around 3,000 people, sat briefly at the very pinnacle of Italian football, the top of Serie A. It seemed to be a football fairytale and the world's media wasted no time latching on to an amazing story. However, when Tim Parks, an English writer living in Verona, wrote his column for *The Guardian* that week, it was decidedly anti-Chievo.

Parks, a fan of Hellas Verona, the more established Verona side, wrote against what he saw as a victory for self-righteous piety and political correctness over the "mad antagonism" which makes Italian football exciting. Parks hit out at the sudden popularity of a club whose peaceful values he didn't see as representing the Italian population. Chievo have a song written for them by a local pop star. 'Gente che vale…gente speciale' it goes: *people who matter, special people*. Parks'

defence of the forthright racism which goes on every week at Hellas games (see Books, p229) is very thin (he claims that it is ironic and theatrical, and that, besides, people need to get these things out of their systems).

Where his explanation rings true, however, is that fanatical, sometimes brutal, partisanship is endemic in Italian football, and in Italian society, too. When the article was translated into Italian and published in the Italian press it created instant controversy, and Parks was derided by many, including the mayor of Verona, who made a public statement against him.

Hellas Verona have since been relegated to Serie B, while Chievo continue to jostle with the big boys near the top of Serie A. In their first season in the top flight they were fifth, behind Juventus, Roma, Inter and Milan, and qualified for the UEFA Cup. In the 2002-2003 season they finished seventh.

ageing structure which rarely fills up, hosted some matches in the 1990 World Cup.

Stadio Bentegodi, piazzale Olimpia, *Map 1, F/G1, p250*

AC Chievo Verona, via Galvani 3, **T** 045 575779, **F** 045 562298, www.chievoverona.it

Hellas Verona, tickets: Verona Point, via Cristofoli 30, **T** 045 575005, **F** 045 577377, www.hellasverona.it *Mon-Sat 0900-1230, 1500-1900. Map 1, F1, p250*

Gyms

Energym, via San Vitale 19, **T** 045 596771, energymverona@yahoo.it *Mon-Fri 0900-2130, Sat 0900-1800. Map 1, D7, p250* A modern, well-equipped gym with courses in everything from kick-boxing and karate to aerogym and 'funkyfun'. Non-members pay € 7.50 to get in, but there are better deals for weekly and fortnightly passes.

Sailing

Torbole (see p90) is one of the best places on Lake Garda for sailing, both for winds and facilities, though Malcesine also has sailing schools, as does Riva.

Circolo Vela Torbole, via Lungolago Verona 6, Torbole, **T** 0464 506240, **F** 0464 505350, www.circolovelatorbole.com

Skiing

The skiing season at San Giorgio (see p95), above Bosco Chiesanuova, has been worryingly short in some recent years, with good snow in short supply. If this is the case, however, it's easy to get further north, and higher up, to resorts such as Folgaria. A bus runs up to the resorts from Porto Nuova station every Sunday morning (early) from Christmas until Easter.

Swimming

Verona's municipal pools (see p68) are excellent, with two olympic-sized pools and two junior pools. The complex at Caldiero (see p97) is similarly well-equipped, with the added bonus of two medieval pools, still in operation, as well as supposedly healing spa waters. Lake Garda also has plenty of good swimming opportunities, such as at Baia delle Sirene (see p85). The waters of the lake are not always as harmless as they seem, however, and there was a spate of drownings in 2003.

Walking

Verona's surroundings offer a wide range of walking possibilities, from gentle strolls among the vines and olive groves of the hills immediately to the north of the river, to full-blown *vie di Ferro* in the Dolomites. Good areas are the hills to the west of Lake Garda (see p83) and the Parco Naturale Regionale della Lessinia (see p91)

Windsurfing

Torbole, on the eastern side of Lake Garda, is almost entirely given over to windsurfing, and important international competitions are held here. It's also a good place to learn, with good winds and enough other people tottering around in the water to stop you feeling foolish.

Surf Segnana Windsurf, via Foci del Sarca, Torbole, **T** 0464 505963, **F** 0464 505498, www.surfsegnana.it

Northern Italian attitudes to homosexuality may be superficially open and accepting, but underneath prejudice can run fairly deep, and much of gay life in Verona, as in the rest of Italy, is hidden from the public eye. The strength of the old fashioned family unit, as well as catholicism and political conservatism, mean that Verona is never likely to become a stronghold of gay society in Italy. However, a lively and active association, Circolo Pink, makes sure that there are always some things happening, be it social events or political activism. There are very few exclusively gay locations in the city itself, although nearby Lake Garda has a much more active gay life.

If there is a gay area of town, it is east of the river in Veronetta, particularly along via XX Settembre towards Porta Vescovo, where the city's sauna can be found. The trendiest gay location in the city is probably Café Bukowski, right in the centre. It is, despite the name, more disco than café.

Associations

Circolo Pink, via Scrimiari 7, **T** 045 8065911,
www.circolopink.it *Map 2, I8, p252* A gay, lesbian and bisexual
'cultural and initiative' organization, Circolo Pink organizes weekly
events and social occasions, including film evenings and 5-a-side
tournaments on Monday evenings, Friday evenings and Saturday
afternoons. On alternate Sunday evenings there are supper
excursions to restaurants and MALA-PINK evenings at the
Malacarne Social Club, (via San Vitale 14, **T** 045 8015203,
Map 1, D7, p250). The organization also participates in
anti-establishment events such as an anti-Christmas Christmas
dinner ("End compulsory consumption! Ban Christmas!")

Beaches

Punta San Viglio To the north of the Baia delle Sirene (see p85)
there is a stretch of beach which is unofficially nudist (la
spiaggia naturista) and has also become one of Lake Garda's
main gay locations.

Clubs and bars

Caffè Bukowski, (see also p168) via Amanti 6, no **T**. *Mon, Wed-Sun
1900-0200*. *Map 2, H7, p252* Not an exclusively gay bar, but with
enough camp disco attitude to ensure a certain proportion of gay
clientele, Bukowski is right in the centre of the old town.

Romeo's Club, via Campofiore. **T** 338 4037781/ **T** 338 1866150,
www.romeosclub.it *Tue-Sat 2300-0530*. *Map 1, E7, p250* Romeo's
is a steadfastly gay location.

Art Club, via Mantova 1/a, Desenzano del Garda, **T** 030 9991004, **F** 030 9120421, www.artclubdisco.com *Wed, Fri, Sat 2330-0500. Wed and Fri €12, Sat €18.* On Lake Garda, Art Club is the area's smartest gay club, though its stylishness occasionally gives it the look of a posh hotel. Minimal amounts of glitter, wavy lines and live music every Wednesday and Saturday from 2300 until 0200.

MALA-PINK, see under Associations, above.

Phonelines

Linea Amica, **T** 045 8012854, *Tue and Thu 2100-2300, Sat 1600-1800*, lineamicagl@tiscalinet.it Gay and lesbian help and advice.

Saunas

The City Sauna, via Giolfino 12, **T** 045 520009. *Map 1, F9, p250* Verona's only sauna, and one of its few established gay locations, east of the city centre.

Kids

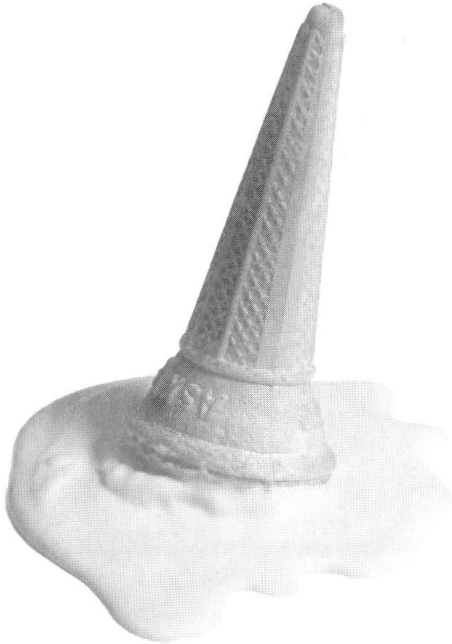

A diet of churches and monuments might test the patience of most children, though most will probably be impressed by the Arena and the Teatro Romano. It would be hard to go far wrong with a climb up the Torre dei Lamberti either. Of the city's museums, few cater particularly well for kids, though the Centro Internazionale di Fotografia has the advantage of being underground in the Roman excavations under the centre of the city. Juliet's balcony and tomb will appeal to some, especially once they are acquainted with the story. A night at the opera can be a long one, but can also be spectacular. Castles proliferate, both in and around the city and natural attractions such as mountains and the lake are always another possibility. In summer, swimming is an excellent option, with several good choices. Bosco Chiesanuova has a big outdoor ice-skating rink, open all year round, which provides another alternative to the ubiquitous theme park. Food shouldn't be too much of a problem, and kids are welcome in nearly all restaurants.

Parks

Impianti Sport Ricreativi Corte del Duca, vicolo Borgo Tascherio. *0900-1200, 1530-1900. Free. Kids must be accompanied by an adult. Map 1, C7, p250* On the left bank of the river is this playground with swings, a roundabout, a small adventure playground, table tennis tables, a wendy house, a football pitch and a bike track.

Parco Giardino Sigurtà (see p98) A mini-train and a mini-castle in a large park with plenty of grass to play on, bikes to hire and sprinklers to run around under. The whole place has a sense of magic about it, and would make a fantastic location for some extended games of hide and seek.

Swimming

As long as getting over the potential fashion faux pas of swimming hats isn't too great a hurdle, the city has an excellent choice of pools. Verona's municipal pools are excellent, and cater to all ages and abilities in an attractive complex (see p68). For equally good pools with a little more history thrown in, Caldiero (see p97) has medieval pools still in use, as well as more standard modern alternatives; or there's always the lake. Baia delle Sirene (see p85) is one of the best swimming places, and would make a good day-trip.

Theme parks

Gardaland is Italy's best known theme park, and has all the usual attractions: rollercoasters, rides, queues and opportunities to get wet and spend lots of money. For more in the way of water, for less in the way of price, Parco Acquatico Cavour is a reasonable alternative.

Kids

Parco Acquatico Cavour, Ariano, Valeggio sul Mincio, **T** 045 7950904, www.parcoacquaticocavour.it *By car, take the exit for Valeggio sul Mincio off the A4 autostrada. By public transport get a taxi from Valeggio sul Mincio. Daily from last Sun in May to 1st Sep, 0930-1900. Mon-Fri €10, Sat-Sun and all of Aug €12* A waterpark complete with an artificial beach, water slides, beach volleyball courts, and clowns.

Gardaland, Castelnuovo del Garda (between Lazise and Peschiera), **T** 045 6449777, **F** 045 6401267, www.gardaland.it *Mid-Jun-mid-Sep, 0900-2400. End of Mar-mid Jun, mid-late Sep, and Oct weekends, daily 0930-1800. €22 a day, kids under 10 €18.50, kids under a metre tall free.* Italy's biggest theme park, on the southern banks of Lake Garda, attracts over three million visitors a year. In the 46 ha of amusements there are 11 shows a day, five restaurants, a medieval joust, Jungle Rapids (where you're likely to get soaked), real dolphins, real poodles, a not-so-real English village, Space Vertigo, where you are carried up and dropped from a great height, an 'island' which flies 50 m into the air, a 2:1 scale model of the Abu Simbel temple in Egypt, dinosaurs and, of course, a rollercoaster. You can get a wanted poster with your picture printed on it, or you could visit the medieval shop and buy lots of weaponry that you wouldn't be allowed to take on the plane home. There's a free bus from Peschiera del Garda train station, or bus 62-64 takes about 35 minutes from Verona station.

Other

Malcesine's revolving cable car will impress most with its size, speed and views, if not necessarily with the speed of its revolutions (see p85). Once at the top of the mountain, wildlife which may be spotted includes eagles and deer. And in winter there is the added bonus of snow.

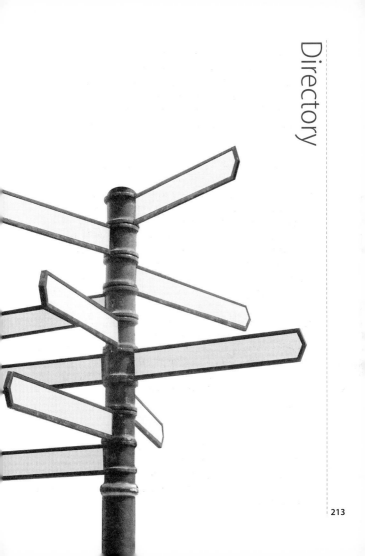

Directory

Airline offices
Ryanair, **T** 889 889973 www.ryanair.com **Alitalia**, **T** 081 7093333, www.alitalia.it **British Airways**, **T** 848 812266, www.britishairways.com

Banks and ATMs
Verona has plenty of bank machines which take Cirrus, Visa and Mastercards. Paying directly with Cirrus cards is less easy, though most larger and tourist-orientated places take credit cards.

Bicycle hire
Pedal Scaligeri has a stand just off piazza Bra at the beginning of via Roma. Prices start at € 3.50 for an hour, € 5 for two hours, plus one euro for each successive hour. Mountain bikes and tandems are also available at a slightly higher price. **T** 333 5367770.

Car hire
Most companies have offices at the airports and at the station. **AVIS**, station: **T** 045 8000663, Verona airport: **T** 045 987571, Brescia airport: **T** 030 9657001; **Europcar**, station: **T** 045 592759, Verona airport **T** 045 8600477, Brescia airport: **T** 030; **Hertz**, station: **T** 045 8000832, Verona airport **T** 045 0458619042, Brescia airport **T** 030 9657302; **Maggiore** (Budget), station: **T** 045 8004808, Verona airport: **T** 045 8619038, Brescia airport: **T** 030 9657298; **Sixt**, Verona airport: **T** 045 8619061.

Credit card lines
There is a single free telephone line for losses of all major types of credit card: **T** 800 207167.

Dentists
Chemists or hotels should be able to provide you with the name and number of a local English-speaking doctor or dentist.

Disabled
Disabled access across the city has improved, but is still often poor, and many old buildings, especially churches, are hard to adapt to wheelchairs. Most museums are accessible, however. Buses are also now accessible (both urban and suburban), though taxis are not. The city council, along with GALM (Gruppo Animazione Lesionati Midollari, via Camacici 4, **T/F** 045 9251241) publish the *Guida Alla Accessibile Verona*, with detailed information in Italian on accessibility and facilities for the disabled in the city.

Doctors
Chemists or hotels should be able to provide you with the name and number of a local English-speaking doctor or dentist.

Electricity
The standard system is 220V, compatible with most UK and US appliances as long as you bring a continental adaptor.

Embassies and consulates
Foreign embassies are in Rome, though Britain and America both also have consulates in Milan, and Canada has a consulate in Padova. **British Consulate** (Consolato Generale Britannico), via San Paolo 7, 20121 Milano, **T** 02 723001, **F** 02 72020153, commreg@milan.mail.fco.gov.uk   **American Consulate** (Consolato Generale Americano), via Principe Amedeo 2/10, 20121 Milano, **T** 02 290351, **F** 02 29001165. **Canadian Consulate** (Consolato Generale Canadese), Riviera Ruzante 25 , Padova, **T** 049 8764833.

Emergency numbers
Police (carabinieri) **T** 113, Fire **T** 115, Ambulance **T** 118,
Breakdowns **T** 803 116.

Hospitals
Ospedale Civile Maggiore, piazzale A Stefani 1, Borgo Trento, **T** 045 8071111.

Internet/email
Verona has three good internet cafés, all in the centre of the city.
FNAC (see p192) also has four terminals, and various cafés offer
web access, including **Square**, where it is free.

Internetfast.it, via Oberdan 16/b, **T** 045 8033212. *Mon-Fri
1000-2200, Sat 1000-2000, Sun 1400-2000. €1.50 per 15 mins.
Map 2, H3, p252* Drinks also available.

Internet etc, via 4 Spade 3/b, **T** 045 8000222, www.internetetc.it
*Sun and Mon 1430-2000, Tue-Sat 1030-2000. 15 minutes €1.60, 30
minutes €2.60, 1 hour €5. Map 2, H5, p252* Plenty of computers,
and they rent out digital cameras and will transfer digital photos
onto CD. Drinks are available, too.

Internettrain, via Roma 17, **T** 045 8013394, **F** 045 8048035.
Map 2, J2, p252 Mon-Fri 1100-2200, Sat and Sun 1400-2000. Card
system where you buy a card which can then be re-charged: 15
minutes €2, 30 minutes €2.50, one hour €5. Credit can also
be used across the road at Bar Roma. 16 terminals and a position
near piazza Bra means Internettrain is often busy, but the system
is efficient.

Language schools
LINGUA IT, via Anfiteatro 10, **T** 045 597975, **F** 045 8048728
www.lingua.it *Map 2, I4, p252* Prices start at €150 for a 20-hour
week of lessons near the Arena. Teachers take students on tours of
the city and accompany them to the opera. Intensive weekend
courses can also be organized, as can cooking courses.

IDEA VERONA, stradone Provolo 16, **T** 045 8015352,
www.ideaverona.com *Map 2, E3, p252* 100 hours of intensive
Italian in four weeks. Courses in cooking, wine and fresco painting
are also possible.

Left luggage
There is a left luggage office at the station. Most hotels will be
happy to look after luggage for you for the day after you check out.

Lost property
On city buses, **T** 045 8005825. On trains, **T** 045 8093827. Otherwise
contact the police, (Vigili Urbani) **T** 8078411.

Libraries
BIblioteca Municipale, via Cappello 43, **T** 045 8079710. *Mon-Fri
0830-1830, Sat and Jul-Aug 0830-1330. Map 2, G6, p252*

Media
Arena is the city's daily newspaper and covers both local and
national events. Two free daily papers, *Città* and *Leggo* are
distributed freely. Neither has much substance, but they can be
useful for checking weather forecasts.

Pharmacies (late night)

Identified by a large green cross outside. There is a rotation of pharmacies which are open outside normal hours. **T** 1100 for addresses of three nearest open pharmacies.

Police

You can always speak to an operator in English on the emergency number **T** 112. The police station is at via del Pontiere 32, **T** 045 8078458.

Post offices

piazza Viviani 7, **T** 045 8051111.

Public holidays

In August, as in much of the rest of Italy, many Veronese abandon the city and head for the seaside. With the opera season in full flow, however, most shops and restaurants remain open, though places off the tourist trail may still close for the month.

Most shops and museums etc will be closed on the days listed. Public transport may run on a Sunday timetable, but is suspended altogether on Christmas Day, New Year's Day, Easter Sunday and May 1st.

1 January: *Capodanno*, New Year's Day. **6 January**, *Befana*, Epiphany. **Easter**: *Pasquetta*, Easter Monday. **25 April**: *Festa della Liberazione*, Liberation Day. **1 May**: *Festa del Lavoro*, Labour Day. **15 August**: *Ferragosto*, Feast of the Assumption. **1 November**: *Ognissanti*, All Saints Day. **8 December**: *L'Immacolata*, Feast of the Immaculate Conception. **25 December**: *Natale*, Christmas Day. **26 December**: *Santo Stefano*, Boxing Day.

Taxi firms
Radiotaxi, **T** 045 532666, 24 hours. There are taxi ranks at the station, in piazza Erbe and in piazza Bra. For costs see p25.

Telephone
In Italy it's now necessary to use area codes no matter where you phone from. Hence you need to dial the code for Verona (045) even from within the city. Numbers in this book are given with the code. To call Italy from abroad you no longer drop the initial '0' of the code as you do for other countries. To call home from Italy dial 00 plus the country code (UK 44, Australia 61, Canada/USA 1, Irish Republic 353) before dialling the number. The **Europa** phone card is excellent value for phoning home. Available from tabacchi (ask for "*una scheda col codice Europa*") it gives you 3 hours of calls anywhere in Europe or America for just € 5. Careful using it with mobiles though – your phone company may charge you for the usually freephone 800 number it uses. Most public phones use **Telecom Italia** cards rather than coins. The cheapest card is € 5. Mobiles with international roaming activated will work, but prices are high both to make and receive calls.

Time
Italy uses **Central European Time**, one hour ahead of Greenwich Mean Time. Daylight saving comes into operation in the summer in synch with the rest of Europe.

Tipping
Tips are generally appreciated but not expected. Nobody will be offended if you don't tip them, though you may find you'll get better service if you do, and it's commonplace to round up bills and not to collect small change.

Toilets

There are (paying) public toilets in piazza Bra and the cortile Mercato Vecchio. Other toilets are few and far between, so make use of those in cafés, bars, restaurants, museums and stations.

Transport enquiries

AMT (Orange city buses) **T** 045 8871111, www.amt.it
APT (Blue suburban buses) **T** 045 8057811, www.apt.vr.it
Ferrovie dello Stato (Trains) **T** 045 892021, www.trenitalia.com

Travel agents

Verona has hundreds of travel agents, any of whom can book flights and most of whom can also organize tours etc. Viaggi Valpantena, right on piazza Bra, is one of the many which are centrally located. Viaggi Valpantena, piazza Bra 20, **T** 045 8009255, **F** 045 8000422.

A sprint through history

7th century BC	A primitive settlement, probably of Rhaetians, exists near the hill of San Pietro, possibly with a ford across the river approximately where Ponte Pietra is now. This is taken over by the Veniti.
216 BC	Verona helps the Romans at the battle of Cannae.
148 BC	The building of the via Postumia, connecting Genoa in the west to Aquileia in the east, makes Verona strategically and economically important.
87 BC	Catullus, the lyrical poet, is born in or near Verona.
49 BC	Verona becomes a municipium, gaining full Roman citizenship.
1st century BC	The city's Roman road structure, which still exists today, is laid out across the area within the bend in the Adige. To the south and west, city walls are built, including the Porta Borsari and Porta dei Leoni.
1st century AD	Growing in importance and wealth, large public buildings are erected, such as the Arena and the amphitheatre, both outside the city walls.
265 AD	Emperor Gallienus builds a new section of city wall, extending the city centre and enclosing the Arena.
4th century	San Zeno, a North African and an enthusiastic angler, becomes the eighth bishop of the city. He later becomes Verona's patron saint.
489 AD	Theodoric, king of the Barbarian Ostrogoths, takes Verona on his way to uniting the peninsula and becoming king of Italy. Contrary to their destructive reputation, the Ostrogoths preserve

much of Roman Verona, repairing the accqueduct and rebuilding parts of the city walls. Theodoric's power base is Ravenna but he has a close attachment to Verona and he builds a palace on the hill of San Pietro. In Germany he is known as 'Theodoric of Verona'.

569   Alboin, king of the Lombards, conquers the city and Verona becomes the capital of his kingdom. Some say that he is eventually assassinated by his wife after he forces her to drink from her father's skull.

774   The Franks succeed the Lombards. Charlemagne's son Pépin makes Verona his seat of power. The city's cultural and political life is reinvigorated.

888   In the aftermath of the disintegration of Charlemagne's empire Verona remains loyal to the German emperors.

1107   Verona makes a commercial treaty with Venice.

1117   An earthquake destroys many of the city's buildings and damages many others, including the Arena, whose outer ring is mostly destroyed.

12th century   Verona becomes a self-governing *comune*: the church, the nobility and the citizens run their own city. Frederick I, Holy Roman Emperor, is displeased by this autonomy and all over Italy conflict ensues between Guelfs (supporters of independent *comunes* and the Pope) and Ghibellines (supporters of the empire). It is against this backdrop of conflict and squabbling between families that Romeo and Juliet is set. An uneasy compromise is reached by the end of the century with the *comunes* acknowledging the overall authority of the Empire, but retaining civic power themselves.

1232 Ezzelino III da Romano, chief justice of Verona and, by all accounts, a thug, crosses to the Ghibellines and rules Verona as a bloody dictator, with support from the Emperor. He also takes control of Vicenza, Padua and Treviso.

1245 Holy Roman Emperor Frederick II spends a month in the city, accompanied by his private zoo of an elephant, five lions and 24 camels.

1262-1387 After Ezzelino's death the della Scala or 'Scaligeri' family rule Verona. Communal government is retained, but the period is, in fact, one of dynasty. From unclear origins, the family takes the city through what is generally seen as its most glorious time and build some of its grandest buildings. Verona becomes the Northern Italian capital of Gothic art and architecture. Dante, Boccaccio and Giotto all stay at the della Scala court of Cangrande, the most successful leader of the era. Many of the della Scala leaders are harsh and ruthless but Cangrande's reputation is that of an intelligent and cultured man.

1387 Gian Galeazzo Visconti, ruler of Milan, forms an alliance with Padua and takes control of Verona.

1390 The Veronesi, resentful of Milanese rule, rise up and expel the government, only to suffer the subsequent sacking of the city in revenge.

1405 Verona bows to the inevitability of Venetian rule and voluntarily cedes power to Venice. Although guilds and statutes are upheld and respected, the most powerful positions go to Venetians and the podestà, or chief justice, has complete powers over law and order. A system of public education, available to all classes, is set up.

1454 Venice signs a peace treaty with Milan, enabling the Veronese aristocracy to start to build undefended country villas and to invest more in agriculture

1500 The population of the city is around 42,000, double that of 50 years before, swollen by successful wool, silk and agricultural industries.

1508 The League of Cambrai, an alliance between France, the Papacy and Habsburg Germany, defeats Venice at the Battle of Agnadello. Verona, still with emotional and historical connections to Germany, accepts the army of German Emperor Maximilian I.

1518 Venice regains control of the city and, in order to shore up defences, it destroys all buildings within a mile of the city walls. Porta Vescovo and Porta San Giorgio are rebuilt.

1530 The city wall is extended further to the south. Three new gates are built between now and 1547.

1630 The plague halves the city's population.

1797 The Napoleonic army defeats the Venetian Republic and Verona is ceded to the Austrian Empire.

1801 The Treaty of Luneville divides Verona between the Austrians and the French. The left bank is controlled by the Austrians, the right bank by the French. The French destroy the Castel San Pietro before ceding ground to the Austrians.

1805	Verona is united again under the Napoleonic government.
1814	Verona becomes part of the Habsburg Empire. The Congress of the Holy Alliance is held in the city in 1822.
1866	Verona joins a newly unified Italy.
1882	A terrible flood destroys two bridges (the Ponte Nuovo and the Ponte Aleardi) and hundreds of houses.
1913	Verdi's Aida is performed for the first time in the Arena.
1939-45	The Second World War allied bombing destroys much of the city, including the Biblioteca Capitolare and damages churches including San Lorenzo. Before retreating the Germans blow up all the city's bridges.
1985	Hellas Verona win Serie A to become Italian football champions.
2003	The public burying of the hatchet between Italian and German leaders Berlusconi and Schroeder takes place in the city after an invitation from Verona's mayor, though the Italian Prime Minister does not turn up at the opera for the first planned meeting. The initial row follows Berlusconi's injudicious comments about Nazis in the European parliament, and a junior Italian minister's description of German tourists as beer-swilling louts who invade Italy every summer.

Art and architecture

148 BC	The opening of the via Postumia paves the way for an enormous amount of Roman building over the next few hundred years. The road crosses the Adige over Ponte Pietra.
1st century AD	The Arena and the theatre are both built. The enormous amphitheatre is initially outside the city walls.
5th-6th centuries	New churches are built in the city, some using the foundations of Roman temples.
Late 8th century	The church of San Zeno, dedicated to the city's patron saint, is built.
1172	The Torre dei Lamberti is built. The city has approximately 70 towers, of which very few survive. These are built by families, partly as a means of defence, partly as symbols of wealth and power. Twenty-two years later it is incorporated into the Palazzo del Comune (town hall), which is built facing onto both piazza Erbe and piazza dei Signori.
1262-1387	Under the Scaligeri dynasty, Verona becomes the Northern Italian capital of Gothic art and architecture and many important buildings are erected.
15th century	Verona, at this point relatively weak and poor, holds on longer to its Gothic style of art and architecture than most other Italian cities, happy to look back on the glorious Scaligeri period rather than to embrace, and pay for, the new style of the Renaissance from the Tuscan south.

1476-92	Verona's finest Renaissance building, the Loggia del Consiglio, is built in piazza dei Signori.
1508	Palladio, the area's most influential architect, is born in Padua.
16th century	Once it accepts the Renaissance, Verona begins to glory in its Roman past, a pride unavailable to its rival Venice, lacking as the Venetian city is in Roman foundations.
	The Venetians adapt existing Scaligeri buildings, adding Renaissance extensions and details to Gothic and Romanesque buildings, such as the octagonal tower on the top of the Torre dei Lamberti. With more painted façades than any other Italian city, Verona is known as *urbs picta*, or the painted city. A trend in building private chapels and altarpieces in existing churches in order to gain social prestige and eternal salvation means that many windows are covered over with enormous paintings. Titian paints the Assumption for the Duomo.
1530s and 40s	Michele Sanmicheli, Verona's most important architect, designs the new city fortifications, including three new gates to the south of the city centre: Porta Nuova (1533), Porta San Zeno (1542) and Porta Palio (1547). He also creates a new street, the grand Corso Porta Nuova, and designs the Canossa and Bevilacqua palaces.
1732	The Teatro Filarmonico, designed by Bibiena, is inaugurated. It is one of Europe's grandest, but is destroyed by fire a mere 17 years later.

1828	The grand Cimitero Monumentale, the city's cemetery, is designed by Giuseppe Barbieri.
1833	The Austrians rebuild the city's defences, adding new fortifications.
1835-48	The Gran Guardia Nuova, designed by Barbieri, is built, closing off a side of piazza Bra.
1864	The iron Ponte Garibaldi becomes the first bridge to have been built in the city since the time of the Scaligeri.
1869-1890	A program of restoration, now seen as clumsy, smartens up many of the city's buildings and monuments, including San Zeno and the Loggia del Consiglio.
1882	Following the famous flood, buildings along the left bank of the river are demolished, and defensive walls are built.
1920	The FIAT garage in via Manin is built by Ettore Fagiuoli. Fagiuoli, born in Verona in 1884, is the city's greatest 20th-century architect.
1924	The Jewish ghetto, to the south of piazza Erbe, is destroyed.
1950s	Ponte Pietra and the Ponte di Castelvecchio are both rebuilt using original materials, following their destruction by the retreating German army at the end of World War Two.
1957-64	Carlo Scarpa restores and adapts Castelvecchio for use as a museum.

Books

Culture, politics and society

Forden, Sarah, *The House of Gucci* (2001), HarperCollins.
Forden's look at the life of Maurizio Gucci, the last of his family
to run the Italian fashion giant, is an extraordinary tale of
money, murder and expensive handbags.

Jones, Tobias, *The Dark Heart of Italy* (2003), Faber and Faber.
Jones's fascinating and readable book goes deeper into the
essence of modern Italy than most books on
the country, examining the violence, the corruption, crime and
(the lack of) punishment, and how Silvio Berlusconi manages
to own or run almost everything.

Sciascia, Leonardo, *The Moro Affair* (2001), Granta Books.
Sciascia, better known as a writer of crime fiction, looks at
the real-life events surrounding the gang murder in 1978
of former Italian Prime Minister Also Moro.

Fiction and travelogue

Parks, Tim, *Europa* (1997), Minerva. Shortlisted for the
Booker Prize, Parks's novel about a love, hate and a three-day
coach journey across Europe was loosely based on a real coach
journey undertaken by lecturers and students of Verona
University (see p16).

Parks, Tim, *Italian Neighbours* (1992), Vintage. The book that
launched Tim Parks is an account of his first ten years living
and working in Verona. Filled with Veronese characters and
their Italian habits, it is an amusing and acutely-observed

insight into ex-pat Italian life. In the follow-up, Italian Education, Parks concentrates on the growing up of his two children.

Parks, Tim, *A Season With Verona* (2002), Vintage.
Following Hellas Verona for a season around the grounds and cities of Serie A football, Parks gets inside the fanatical mentality of Verona supporters and all their rivalries and discriminations, especially against the south and against black players, but also against the other Verona side, Chievo (see also box, 'The two teams of Verona', p202). He also gets to travel the country and give an insight into its beautiful, exciting, and frustrating national sport.

Food and drink

Ferrigno, Ursula, *Truly Italian* (1999), Mitchell Beazley. If you want to recreate some of Verona's Italian food without so much of the horsemeat and bone marrow, Ursula Ferrigno's vegetarian Italian cookbook is one of the best introductions. With separate sections including pasta, risotto, bread and salads, all beautifully illustrated, the book is crammed full of simple but delicious Italian recipes.

Guy, Patricia, *Amarone*, Morganti Editore. A small hardback book, Guy's guide to Verona's best wine is also an attractive and colourful introduction to the Valpolicella area.

History

Farrell, Nicholas, *Mussolini* (2003), Weidenfeld & Nicholson.
Farrell's biography of the much reviled and much ridiculed fascist dictator takes an unexpectedly positive view of his early career but pulls no punches when it comes to his later devastating mistakes. A portrait of the man as much of as the leader, it gives an interesting insight into a personality which, for a while at least,

seduced Italy. It also covers the period of the Salò Republic, when Mussolini's powerbase was on the shores of Lake Garda (see p88).

Ruskin, John, *Verona and its Rivers* (1870), Bonato Editore. Only available in Italy as a slim volume in both English and Italian, this was a lecture given by Ruskin to the Royal Institution, which, in few pages, covers good government, irrigation, rocks and the della Scala family.

Photography

Barbey, Bruno, *The Italians*, Harry N. Abrams, Inc. Barbey's atmospheric black and white photos of Italians (from nuns to prostitutes and mafiosi) in 1960s Italy still epitomise everything that is cool about the country and its people.

Bassotto, Enzo and Raffaello, *Verona: Topographies* (2002), Cierre Edizioni. Wide format black and white panoramic photos of the city, largely unpopulated by people. A modern, spacious and sometimes sideways look at the architecture and the spaces of the city. Hard to find outside Italy.

Romeo and Juliet – a synopsis

The wealthy Capulet and Montague families hate each other. Romeo, son of Lord Montague, goes to a masked party held by Lord Capulet, hoping to see his beloved Rosaline but instead meets another girl, whom he later discovers her to be Juliet, daughter of Lord Capulet. That night Romeo finds Juliet on her balcony. They talk, reveal their love, and agree to marry. The next morning Romeo sends Juliet a message and they are secretly married in Friar Lawrence's cell. They agree to meet in the evening.

That afternoon, however, Romeo becomes involved in a fight between his friend Mercutio and Tybalt, a Capulet, and Juliet's cousin. Tybalt kills Mercutio, and in return Romeo kills Tybalt. Romeo spends the night in the city in Juliet's room, before leaving early in the morning for Mantova.

Lord Capulet, meanwhile, announces that he has found a husband for Juliet, and that she is to be married. Juliet cannot admit that she is already married to a Montague. She goes to Friar Lawrence for help. He suggests she drink a potion which will make her appear dead for 42 hours so that she is put into the family tomb, from where Romeo will take her away. The night before the wedding, Juliet does this, and in the morning she is found, apparently dead.

But news of her 'death' travels faster to Romeo than the messenger sent by the Friar with news of his plan. Romeo buys some poison and hastens to Verona. He breaks open the tomb, finds Juliet's body, swallows the poison and dies. When Juliet awakes and finds Romeo's dead body, she takes his dagger and stabs herself. Friar Lawrence finds the two lovers dead, and, after he recounts the story to Lords Capulet and Montague, they agree to put their quarrels aside, and to be united in their grief.

Language

In hotels and bigger restaurants, you'll usually find English is spoken. The further you go from the tourist centre, however, the more trouble you may have, unless you have at least a smattering of Italian. Around the shores of Lake Garda English, German and Italian are spoken almost equally.

You will also find that the heavy Veronese dialect is spoken, especially as you go out of the city into the surrounding countryside. A slight variant on the Veneto dialect, once the official language of Venice, the dialect spoken today in and around Verona has changed little in centuries and exhibits Germanic influences. Characteristic sounds are short, clipped and nasal, or come from the back of the mouth.

Pronunciation

Stress in spoken Italian usually falls on the penultimate syllable. Italian has standard sounds: unlike English you can work out how it sounds from how it's written and vice versa.

Vowels:

a: like 'a' in cat
e: like 'e' in vet, or slightly more open, like the 'ai' in air (except after c or g, see consonants below)
i: like 'i' in sip (except after c or g, see below)
o: like 'o' in fox
u: like 'ou' in soup

Consonants:

Generally consonants sound the same as in English, though 'e' and 'i' after 'c' or 'g' make them soft (a 'ch' or a 'j' sound) and are silent themselves, whereas 'h' makes them hard (a 'k' or 'g' sound), the opposite to English. So ciao is pronounced 'chaow', but chiesa (church) is pronounced 'kee-ay-sa'.

The combination 'gli' is pronounced like the 'lli' in million, and 'gn' like 'ny' in Tanya.

Basics

thank you *grazie*
hi/goodbye *ciao*
good day (until after lunch/mid-afternoon) *buongiorno*
good evening (after lunch) *buonasera*
goodnight *buonanotte*
goodbye *arrivederci*
please *per favore*
I'm sorry *mi dispiace*
excuse me *permesso*
yes *si*
no *no*

Numbers

one *uno*, two *due*, three *tre*, four *quattro*, five *cinque*, six *sei*, seven *sette*, eight *otto*, nine *nove*, 10 *dieci*, 11 *undici*, 12 *dodici*, 13 *tredici*, 14 *quattordici*, 15 *quindici*, 16 *sedici*, 17 *diciassette*, 18 *diciotto*, 19 *diciannove*, 20 *venti*, 21 *ventuno*, 22 *ventidue*, 30 *trenta*, 40 *quaranta*, 50 *cinquanta*, 60 *sessanta*, 70 *settanta*, 80 *ottanta*, 90 *novanta*, 100 *cento*, 200 *due cento*, 1000 *mille*.

Questions

how? *come?*
how much? *quanto?*
when? *quando?*
where? *dove?*
why? *perché?*
what? *che cosa?*

Problems

I don't understand *non capisco*
I don't know *non lo so*
I don't speak Italian *non parlo italiano*
How do you say …(in Italian)? *come si dice … (in italiano)?*
Is there anyone who speaks English? *c'è qualcuno che parla inglese?*

Shopping

this one/that one *questo/quello*
less *meno*
more *di più*
How much is it/are they? *quanto costa/costano?*
Can I have …? *posso avere …?*

Travelling

one ticket for… *un biglietto per…*
single *solo andate*
return *andate ritorno*
does this go to Mantova? *questo va per Mantova?*
airport *aeroporto*
bus stop *fermata*
train *treno*
car *macchina*
taxi *tassi*

Eating/drinking

what do you recommend? *che cosa mi consegna?*
can I have the bill? *posso avere il conto?*
what's this? *cos'è questo?*
is there a menu? *c'è un menù?*
where's the toilet? *dov'è il bagno?*

Food and drink

acqua frizzante/naturale sparkling/still water
agnello lamb
anguria watermelon
antipasto starter
arancia orange
baccalà salt-cod
birra beer
caffè coffee (ie espresso)
caffè macchiato espresso with a dash of foamed milk
carne meat
coniglio rabbit
coppa/cono cone/cup
formaggio cheese
frutti di mare seafood
funghi mushrooms
gelato ice-cream
granita flavoured crushed ice
insalata salad
manzo beef
melanzane aubergine
olio oil
pandoro Veronese Christmas cake (see p145)
pane bread
pastissàda de caval Veronese horsemeat stew
Pearà Veronese bone marrow sauce
peperoncino chilli pepper
peperone pepper (vegetable)
pesce fish
pollo chicken
polpette meatballs
pomodoro tomato

rucola rocket
vino rosso/bianco red/white wine
vitello veal

Hotels

a double/single room *una camera doppia/singola*
a double bed *un letto matrimoniale*
bathroom *bagno*
Is there a view? *c'è una bella vista?*
Can I see the room? *posso vedere la camera?*
When is breakfast? *a che ora è la colazione?*
Can I have the key? *posso avere la chiave?*

Time

morning *mattina*
afternoon *pommeriggio*
evening *sera*
night *notte*
soon *presto/fra poco*
later *più tardi*
What time is it? *Che ore sono?*
today/tomorrow/yesterday *oggi/domani/ieri*

Days

Monday *lunedi*
Tuesday *martedi*
Wednesday *mercoledi*
Thursday *giovedi*
Friday *venerdi*
Saturday *sabato*
Sunday *domenica*

Conversation

alright *va bene*
right then *allora*
who knows! *bo! / chi sa*
good luck! *in bocca al lupo!* (literally, 'in the mouth of the wolf')
one moment *un'attimo*
hello (when answering a phone) *pronto* (literally, 'ready')
let's go! *andiamo!*
enough/stop *basta!*
give up! *dai!*
I like ... *mi piace ...*
how's it going? (well, thanks) *come va?* (bene, grazie)
how are you? *come sta/stai?* (polite/informal)

Gestures

Italians are famously theatrical and animated in dialogue and use a variety of gestures.

Side of left palm on side of right wrist as right wrist is flicked up
Go away

Hunched shoulders and arms lifted with palms of hands outwards What am I supposed to do?

Thumb, index and middle finger of hand together, wrist upturned and shaking What are you doing/what's going on?

Both palms together and moved up and down in front of stomach Same as above

All fingers of hand squeezed together To signify a place is packed full of people

Front of side of hand to chin 'Nothing', as in 'I don't understand' or 'I've had enough'

Flicking back of right ear To signify someone is gay

Index finger in cheek To signify good food

Index

Credits

Footprint credits

Editors: Alan Murphy, Davina Rungasamy
Map editor: Sarah Sorensen

Publisher: Patrick Dawson
Series created by: Rachel Fielding
Cartography: Robert Lunn, Claire
Benison, Kevin Feeney, Shane Feeney
Proof-reading: Claire Boobbyer
Design: Mytton Williams

Photography credits

Front cover: Julius Honnor (Roman road)
Inside: Julius Honnor (p1 Tomb of
Cangrande I, p5 Audio headset at Juliet's
house, p29 Pillar by Duomo entrance,
p81 Torre dei Tormento in Vicenza)
Generic images: John Matchett
Back cover: Julius Honnor (Printer's
workshop)

Print

Manufactured in Italy by LegoPrint.
Pulp from sustainable forests.

Footprint feedback

We try as hard as we can to make
each Footprint guide as up to date as
possible but, of course, things always
change. If you want to let us know
about your experiences – good, bad
or ugly – then don't delay, go to
www.footprintbooks.com and send
in your comments.

Publishing information

Footprint Verona
1st edition
Text and maps © Footprint Handbooks
Ltd Nov 2003

ISBN 1 903 471 850
CIP DATA: a catalogue record for this
book is available from the British Library

Published by Footprint
6 Riverside Court
Lower Bristol Road
Bath, BA2 3DZ, UK
T +44 (0)1225 469141
F +44 (0)1225 469461
discover@footprintbooks.com
www.footprintbooks.com

Distributed in the USA by
Publishers Group West

Publishing stuff

Complete title list

(P) denotes pocket
Handbook

For a different view…
choose a Footprint

More than 100 Footprint travel guides
Covering more than 150 of the world's most exciting
countries and cities in Latin America, the Caribbean, Africa, Indian
sub-continent, Australasia, North America, Southeast Asia, the
Middle East and Europe.

Discover so much more…
The finest writers. In-depth knowledge. Entertaining and
accessible. Critical restaurant and hotels reviews. Lively
descriptions of all the attractions. Get away from the crowds.

Check out...

WWW...

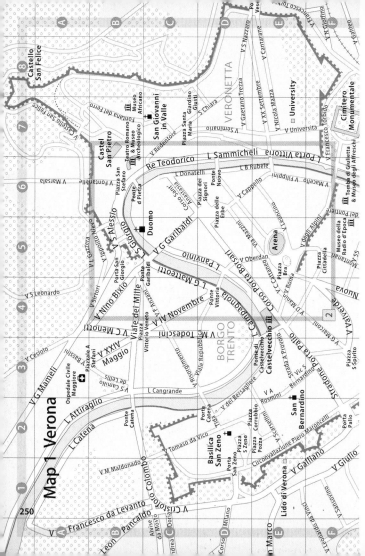

Map 1 Verona

A **B** **C** **D** **E** **F**

8 Castello San Felice

7 V Castello San Felice
Castel San Pietro
Fontana del Ferro
Teatro Romano & Museo Archeologico
San Giovanni in Valle
Museo Africano
VERONETTA
V S Nazzaro
V S Cantarane
V S Mazza
V Gaetano Trezza
V XX Settembre
V Nicola Mazza
Piazza Santa Maria
Giardino Giusti
V S Chiara
University
Cimitero Monumentale
V N Giolfino
V N Giolfino
V Francesco Torbido
V Francesco Torbido

6 V Marsala
V Fontanelle
Piazza San Stefano
Re Teodorico
L Sammicheli
L Porta Vittoria
L Rubele
V Universita
Tomba di Giulietta & Museo degli Affreschi

5 V Galzria
V Ippolito Nievo
V S Alessio
L S Giorgio
Duomo
L Donatelli
Ponte Pietra
Ponte Nuovo
Corso Sant'Anastasia
Piazza dei Signori
Piazza delle Erbe
V Cappello
V A Diaz
del Pontiere
Museo della Radio d'Epoca
V S S Montanari

4 V S Leonardo
Porta San giorgio
V Sartori
V G Garibaldi
L S Giorgio
V Mazzini
L Panvinio
Arena
V degli Alpini
Piazza Citadella
V Nuova

3 V Cesiolo
V G Mameli
Ospedale Civile Maggiore
Piazzale A Stefani
V S Camillo de'lellis
V XXIX Maggio
V A Nino Bixio
Viale del Mille
Piazza Vittorio Veneto
V C Menotti
A IV Novembre
L Campagnola
L G Matteotti
Corso Porta Borsari
Ponte Vittoria
V C Cavanagini
V D Manin
V A Rosmini
V C Cappello
V C Cavour
Piazza Bra
V Roma
V Pallone
V Valverde
Piazza S S Spirito

2 BORGO TRENTO
V M Todeschini
Castelvecchio
Ponte di Castelvecchio
Strada A Provolo
Strada Porta Palio
V S Bernardino
San Bernardino
Porta Palio

1 250
V Francesco da Levanto
Leon B Pancaldo
V Cristoforo Colombo
Alvise da Mosto
Andrea Doria
Corso Milano
San Marco
Lido di Verona
V Galliano
V Giulio
V Vasovnovo
Il Leopardo di Pula

Basilica San Zeno
Piazza S Zeno
Porta San Zeno
V Tomaso da Vico
V.M.Maldonado
L Cangrande
L Attiraglio
L Catena
Ponte Catena
Porta Catena
V del Bersagliere
Piazza Corrubbio
Piazza Pozza
Circonvallazione Piero Maroncelli

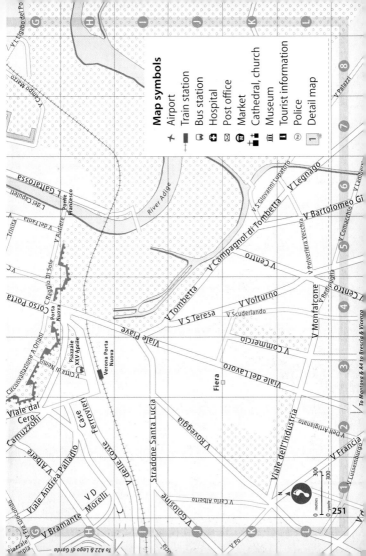

Map symbols

✈	Airport
▮	Train station
◧	Bus station
✚	Hospital
⊠	Post office
⑯	Market
✚	Cathedral, church
ﬧ	Museum
■	Tourist information
②	Police
1	Detail map

251

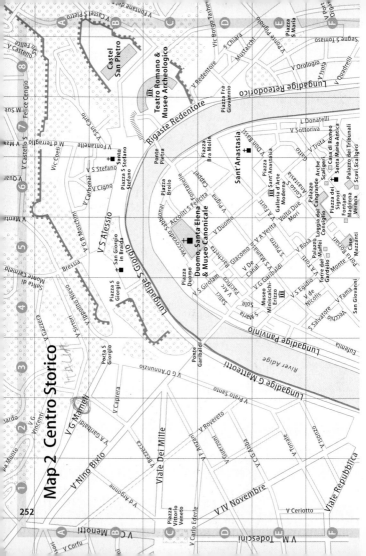

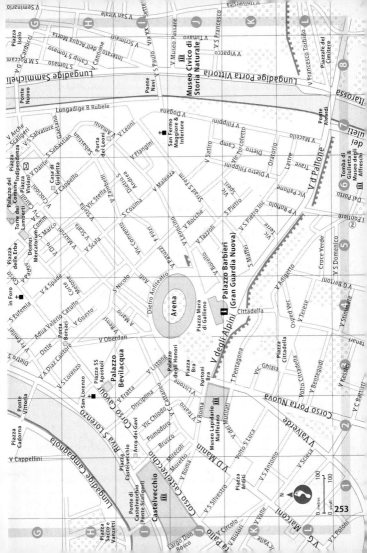

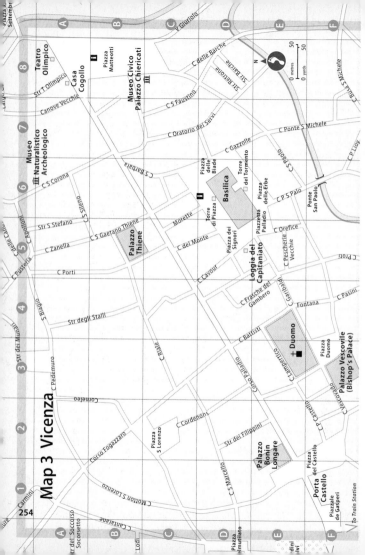

Map 3 Vicenza

254

Teatro Olimpico

Str T Olimpico

Casa Cogollo

Canove Vecchie

Piazza Matteotti

Museo Civico Palazzo Chiericati

Museo Naturalistico Archeologico

C S Corona

C S Stefano

C S Gaetano Thiene

Str S Stefano

C Zanella

C Porti

Palazzo Thiene

Piazza Settembr

V Giuriolo

C delle Barche

Str Retrone

Str Barche

C S Faustino

C Oratorio dei Servi

C Ponte S Michele

C Gazzolle

Piazza delle Biade

Torre del Tormento

Piazza delle Erbe

C S Barbara

Basilica

Morette

Torre di Piazza

Piazzetta Palladio

C Cavour

Piazza dei Signori

C del Monte

Loggia del Capitaniato

C Orefice

C Pescherie Vecchie

C Frasche del Gambero

C Garibaldi

Fontana

C Battisti

Duomo

Piazza Duomo

Palazzo Vescovile (Bishop's Palace)

Str degli Stalli

C Rialto

Corso Palladio

C Lampertico

C Vescovo

C Pedemuro

S Biagio

Corneleo

Cordenons

Str dei Filippini

Piazza S Lorenzo

Corso Fogazzaro

C Motton S Lorenzo

C S Marcello

Palazzo Bonin Longare

Porta del Castello

Piazzale del Castello

Piazzale de Gasperi

To Train Station

Piazza Ammutinato

N

0 metres 50
0 yards 50

C Ponte S Michele

C S Paolo

Ponte San Paolo

Proti

C Pasini

C del Soccorso Soccorsetto

Cantalane

Carmini

Lodi

dini ilvi

A B C D E F

1 2 3 4 5 6 7 8